BOLA AKIN-JOHN

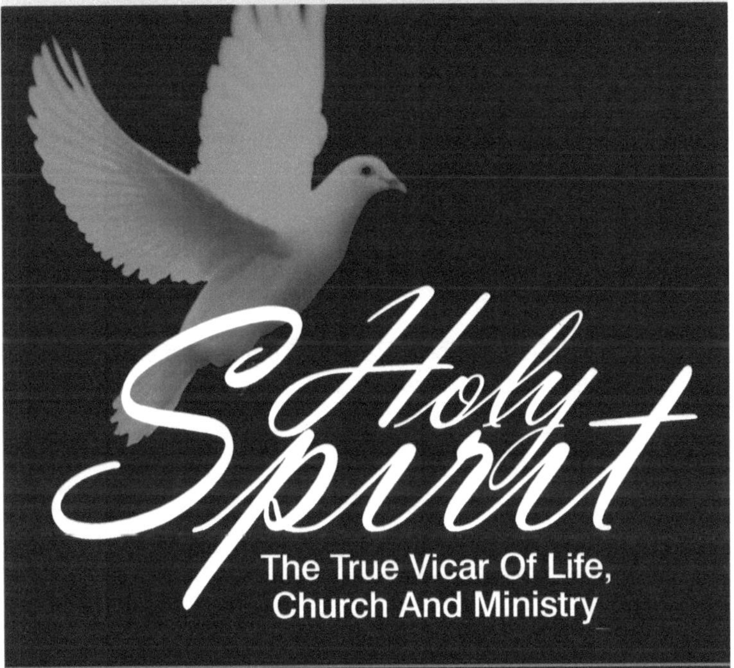

If He doesn't work, **nothing will Work.**
If he doesn't move, **nothing will move**

Published by:

 CHURCH GROWTH SERVICES INC.
Block C, FHA Abesan IV Estate, Mosan Bus Stop, Ipaja, Lagos
Tel.: 234-01-8976100, 08023000714, 08029744296
E-mail: akingrow@yahoo.com Website: churchgrowthafrica.org

Printed in Nigeria by:
LIFE & MINISTRY PUBLICATIONS
Tel.: 234-1-7934133, (0)8037152451

CONTENTS

DEDICATION

Who else is worthy of the dedication of this book
than the
Spirit of Fire;
Spirit of Holiness;
Spirit of God;
Spirit of Resurrection and Life;
Spirit of Kindness and Fear of the Lord.

I praise you forever and ever for who you are and what
you are doing silently in the world.

APPRECIATION

My deepest appreciation goes to the Triune God of Sinai, Calvary and Pentecost for the enablement to finally put this wonderful book together.

I cannot but thank my associates, family and co-workers for their invaluable contribution to our ministry and support all the way. As usual, I'm equally grateful to my editors and printer who did marvelous job of getting out the book in record time.

I sincerely hope the Lord will bring spiritual revolution to the heart, life and ministry of every reader of this book.

Shalom to everyone.

INTRODUCTION

Over the years, it has always been a burden in my heart to write a book on the Person and role of the Holy Spirit in the church. Early in my Christian and ministerial life, I had the privilege of reading; "Holy Spirit, My Senior Partner" by David Yonngi Cho and I was greatly blessed. Few years later, I came across "Good Morning Holy Spirit" by Benny Hinn and it opened my eyes more to the person and work of the Holy Spirit in the life of Christians. In some of our conferences to Pastors and Church Leaders, I have tried to emphasize the prime importance of the Holy Spirit to the growth and health of the church but I have never been truly satisfied.

Then in the last few years, the Lord began to call my attention to a growing trend in the body of Christ: using the Holy Spirit for our selfish ends and seeing Him only as power, anointing and a force. Moreover, once you can speak in some tongues, it is guaranteed that you are filled with the Holy Spirit, even though you are not showing forth any godly fruit in your life.

Furthermore, men, women and churches are rising to the surface who don't reckon with the Holy Spirit. Even in Pentecostal, Evangelical and Charismatic circles. Large numbers of churches know next to nothing about the person and work of the Holy Spirit. Many professed Christians are not filled with the Holy Spirit and large numbers of Pastors are pastoring without any infilling or ongoing relationship with the Holy Spirit. Therefore, many are dabbling into occultic and demonic powers to lead their "churches" today.

There is the story of an acclaimed Pentecostal Pastor, the General Overseer of Divine Justice Church, Owerri, Imo State, South East Nigeria, who was arrested for kidnapping and lots of Indian hemp was found in his church. When he was interviewed, he said; "...some of my members do prepare some delicacies with it, which they serve me. I love Indian hemp because after eating Indian hemp, it gives me inspiration, then when I mount the pulpit, you will notice the efficacy of hemp". (Sun Newspaper, Thursday 16th May 2013, page 35).

Well, this is not an isolated case of pastors preaching under the influence of Indian hemp, alcohol, spirits and wine, but a growing trend, simply because the Holy Spirit has been cast off in their lives and churches. According to Hosea 8:3;

"Israel hath cast off the thing that is good; the enemy shall pursue him."

The enemy is pursuing, catching up and tearing apart the church of God today primarily because the true Vicar of the church – The Holy Spirit is largely unknown, unrecognized and unwelcomed in His church.\

In spite of the Biblical fact that this is the age of the Holy Spirit, yet too many churches and Christians living are devoid of the Person and presence of the Spirit of God today. We love the Father, pray through the name of the Son, but forget the Living Spirit.

As someone who has received grace to share with many church leaders and look the church over with the eyes of the Spirit, this book is my sincere and humble attempt to bring the church back to the Holy Spirit through systematic orientation to the third person of the Trinity. Yes, there are many literatures about the Holy Spirit out there, but with particular emphasis to the church is my major concern in this book. As John Calvin said; "The sin of the Old Testament is the rejection of Jehovah God. The sin of the New Testament is the rejection of God the Holy Spirit".

In most Christian churches, the Spirit is entirely overlooked. He is taken for granted. Whether He is present or absent makes no real difference to anyone. Brief reference is made to Him in the Doxology and Benediction, further than that, He might as well not exist and some churches have completely ignored Him. The only thing majority of professed Christians know about the Holy Spirit is calling down 'Holy Ghost fire' upon our perceived enemies. Though they have cast Him off and thereby open themselves up to the enemy's attacks, yet they often invoke the fire of the Holy Ghost upon their self-made enemies!

The cold, lukewarm, worldly and dead churches today are the outcome of neglecting the Holy Spirit. The large numbers of secular preachers who are devoid of godly spirituality are the sure evidences of lack of the presence and power of the Holy Spirit in some churches. The numerical growth of more goats than sheep in many churches today signifies the abysmally low presence of the Holy Spirit. The unspirituality of the church and carnalities here and there show that the

Holy Spirit has been driven out of the church.

Truth be told, the church cannot escape the Holy Spirit. He is the Vicar of the church. Nothing works without Him. The earlier we repent of our sins of rejecting Him, and welcome Him back to our lives and churches, the better for us. We cannot survive without the mighty Person and presence of the Holy Spirit. We must therefore welcome Him afresh, fellowship, obey and listen to Him anew, because He is God's Executive Agent and Chief Executor of His programmes in the world. Any church or Christian without the Holy Spirit is dead, soundly dead!

I sincerely hope you will allow the Lord to use this book to awaken you and your church to the Person and presence of the Holy Spirit like never before. Then He will make you and your church into what God purposed for you.

Dear Holy Spirit, it's time, visit and sweep over your church afresh!

Francis Bola Akin-John
June 2013.

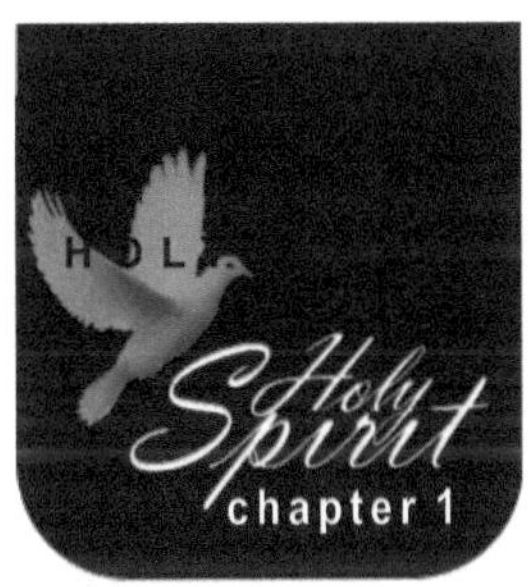

WHO IS THE
HOLY SPIRIT?

The Holy Spirit is the third person of the Trinity. He is part of the God-head. There is one God, but eternally manifested in three distinct Persons. The Holy Spirit is a Person different from the Father and Son, though united to both in the mysterious oneness of the Godhead.

"And Jesus, when he was baptized, went up straightway out of the water: and, lo, the heavens were opened unto him, and he saw the Spirit of God descending like a dove, and lighting upon him:" - Matthew 3:16-17

In this scripture, we see Jesus on earth, the Spirit descending as a dove upon Him and the voice of the Father speaking from heaven. In Acts 7:55-56 also, we saw Stephen witnessing by the power of the Spirit, and Jesus standing up at the right hand of the seated Father in heaven. He is identified with the Father and Son.

"But Peter said, Ananias, why hath Satan filled thine heart to lie to the Holy Ghost, and to keep back part of the price of the land? Whiles it remained, was it not thine own? and after it was sold, was it not in thine own power? why hast thou conceived this thing in thine heart? thou hast not lied unto men, but unto God. Then Peter said unto her, How is it that ye have agreed together to tempt the Spirit of the Lord? behold, the feet of them which have buried thy husband are at the door, and shall carry thee out" – Acts 5:3-4,9

The Hebrew word – 'rauch' in the Old Testament means the Holy Spirit and it appears over 100 times. In the New Testament, the word is 'Pneuma', which means God's essence, God's Spirit and breath of God. The phrase, Holy Ghost and Holy Spirit is used interchangeably in the Bible, especially in the New Testament and they mean the same thing. But personally I prefer the Holy Spirit because He is not a ghost, but a person.

> *The divinity of the Holy Spirit implies that the church is blessed to have His presence and therefore should allow His leadership and direction.*

The Bible, which is the final arbiter in matter of life and experience, clearly shows that divine attributes were used for the Holy Spirit.

He is shown as Omnipresence (Psalm 139:7-10);

Omniscience (I Cor. 2:10-11); Omnipotent (Zechariah 4:6); Eternal (Hebrews 9:14); Creator (Job 33:4) and Sovereign (I Cor. 12:1-11).

His titles includes the Spirit of God (Gen. 1:2); Spirit of the Lord (Luke 4:18); Spirit of our God (I Cor. 6:11); Spirit of the Living God (2 Cor. 3:3); Spirit of Truth (John 14:19); Spirit of life (Romans 8:2); Spirit of wisdom and understanding (Isaiah 11:1-2); Spirit of counsel and might (Isaiah 11:2) and The Comforter (John 14:26).

The divinity of the Holy Spirit implies that the church is blessed to have His presence and therefore should allow His leadership and direction. The major weakness of the Old Testament saints is that the Holy Spirit was not within them. But God gave Him to the New Testament saints to live within us and lead us.

"Then the heathen that are left round about you shall know that I the LORD build the ruined places, and plant that that was desolate: I the LORD have spoken it, and I will do it. Thus saith the Lord GOD; I will yet for this be enquired of by the house of Israel, to do it for them; I will increase them with men like a flock. As the holy flock, as the flock of Jerusalem in her solemn feasts; so shall the waste cities be filled with flocks of men: and they shall know that I am the LORD." – Ezekiel 36:36-38.

Since the Holy Spirit came down fully on the day of Pentecost in Acts 2:1-4, He has not gone back. He is fully here to be the true Vicar - Shepherd, guide, guard and gauge to the individual Christian and the body of Christ. And He will be here till the rapture. However, He will not force Himself on any one or church. If you don't believe in Him and welcome Him into your life, He will never force Himself on you.

THE PERSON
OF THE HOLY SPIRIT

The man whom God used to build the largest church in history, David Yonngi Cho attributes that great work of God to his personal relationship with the Holy Spirit. When he learned about the Divinity and Personhood of the Holy Spirit, he decided to place an empty chair in his Boardroom and asked the Spirit of God to be the Chairman of every meeting and guide in every decision-making. He will invite the Holy Spirit to be the Senior preacher, choose what words to use and what ways to follow. He testified that he has never been disappointed by the Spirit of the Lord.

The Holy Spirit is a pure and an undefiled Spirit; there is no dirtiness or impurity in Him. He is not just a personification of divine energy but a wholesome person. He is not an experience or a thing; rather, He is everything a person should be. Our Lord Jesus, the second person of the Trinity used masculine pronoun for the Holy Spirit in several places (John 14:16-26; John 16:7-15; John 15:26).

A person exhibits the essential characteristics of intellect, feeling and will, so also is the Holy Spirit. He has Will-power (I Cor. 2:11); Intelligence (Neh. 9:20); Feeling (Acts 15:28); Mind (Romans 8:27); Decision (I Cor. 12:9-11); Speaks and hears (Acts 13:2; John 16:13-15).

With all these characteristics, you will see that the Holy Spirit is a wholesome Person that you can relate personally with. He is not just a force to be used or a power to tap into, but a Person that is much more than anointing. Though we cannot see Him with the physical eyes, yet He is real and ever present. Surely, no one has seen the wind with the eye, yet you can sense it, feel it and know its effects on your body, so also is the Holy Spirit.

An individual accomplishes unique work based upon his intellect and will, so also is the Holy Spirit. The Spirit of God Creates (Gen. 1:2); Convicts (John 16:8); Commands (Acts 8:29); Comforts (John 14:26); Teaches (John 16:13) and Intercedes (Romans 8:26). It is only a divine person that can do all these, not an inanimate force.

> *He is not an experience or a thing; rather, He is everything a person should be.*

Furthermore, the Holy Spirit can be given a personal treatment. He can be mistreated or obeyed like the other person of the Godhead. Knowingly or unknowingly, lots of Christians are quenching (I Thess. 5:19); tempting (Acts 5:9); grieving (Eph. 4:30) and vexing (Isaiah 63:10) the Spirit of God today; while some have learnt to fellowship and commune with Him (II Cor. 13:14).

The way you treat the Holy Spirit of God is the way He will respond to you. If you ignore or take Him for granted, then your life and ministry will be dry and fruitless. But if you recognize Him and take time to fellowship with Him and obey His leadings, then you will be alive, living, dynamic and enjoy your walk with God. You cannot really know God without the Holy Spirit. He is the one that will reveal the things of the Lord to you.

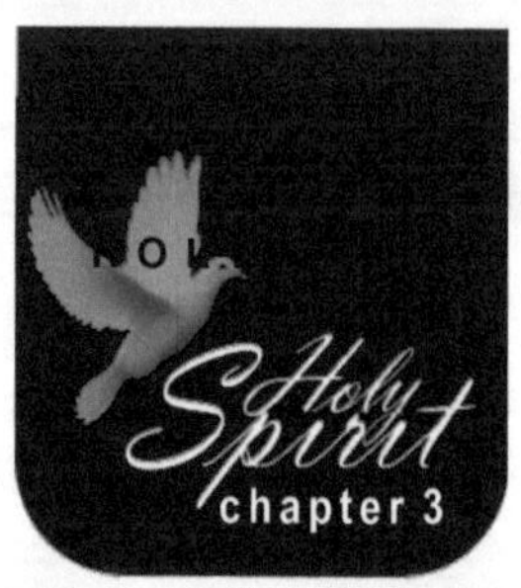

THE SPIRIT
WHICH THE WORLD
CANNOT RECEIVE

"Even the Spirit of truth; whom the world cannot receive, because it seeth him not, neither knoweth him: but ye know him; for he dwelleth with you, and shall be in you." – John 14:17

"But ye are not in the flesh, but in the Spirit, if so be that the Spirit of God dwell in you. Now if any man have not the Spirit of Christ, he is none of his. For as many as are led by the Spirit of God, they are the sons of God. The Spirit itself beareth witness with our spirit, that we are the children of God:" – Romans 8:9, 14, 16.

In my early days of becoming a Christian, we were taught vigorously to pursue the baptism of the Holy Spirit. In fact, if you have not been baptized with the Holy Spirit, you are looked upon as a second class Christian or semi-unbeliever. You will not be allowed to eat the Holy Communion bread; you will not be allowed to join the work force of the church and you are denied many other spiritual experiences. So, I was desperately searching and hungry for the Spirit of God to fill me and indwell my being; for it is then I truly belong to Him. And that is the truth of the scripture. If anyone does not possess the Holy Spirit, he or she doesn't belong to Christ.

> **"But ye are not in the flesh, but in the Spirit, if so be that the Spirit of God dwell in you. Now if any man have not the Spirit of Christ, he is none of his".** – Romans 8:9.

Our Lord Jesus, in promising the Holy Spirit to His disciples said that it is the Spirit which the world cannot receive because the world does not know Him. Herein is the difference then. You can only receive the Holy Spirit if you have truly repented and belonged to the Lord. The Holy Spirit is God possessing our beings and directing our lives; and that will only be possible if you have genuinely repented, turned away from sins and living holy and pure lives. He is exclusively preserved for those who have drawn closer to the Lord.

If you are a lover of the world, wallowing in lusts, immoralities, ungodliness and denying God, you can never have the Spirit of God.

The world with its sinful pleasures, wickedness, corruptions, idol worship and lusts cannot receive the Spirit of God. If you are a lover of the world, wallowing in lusts, immoralities, ungodliness and denying God, you can never have the Spirit of God. And once you don't have His Spirit, you surely don't belong to Him irrespective of your wealth, worth, status, religious activities and moral uprightness.

If you fill your heart with the drunkenness, riches and corruptions of this world, the Spirit of God will have no place in your heart. So long your heart is filled with wickedness, evil thoughts, bitterness, unforgiving spirit, immoralities, lying, deceit and pollutions of this world; you will drive out the Spirit of God from your heart. Once you backslide into immoralities, stealing, idol worship and things that quench the Spirit of God, you no longer belong to Him because the Holy Spirit cannot dwell where these things abound.

Though some preachers and professed Christians speak in tongues today, yet all these works of the flesh are manifesting in their lives. I make bold to say that those tongues are fake tongues from some spirits in the atmosphere, not from the Holy Spirit of God. The Holy Spirit cannot be in you and evil will still have a place in your heart, character and life.

When you manifest the traits of the world in your life, you will be possessed by the spirits of the world. The Holy Spirit is only given to those who belong to Him and once they walk in the spirit, their characters and lives will show forth Christ-likeness. When you receive His Spirit, He will overshadow you daily to produce Christ in you and destroy all the works of the world in you (Luke 1:36).

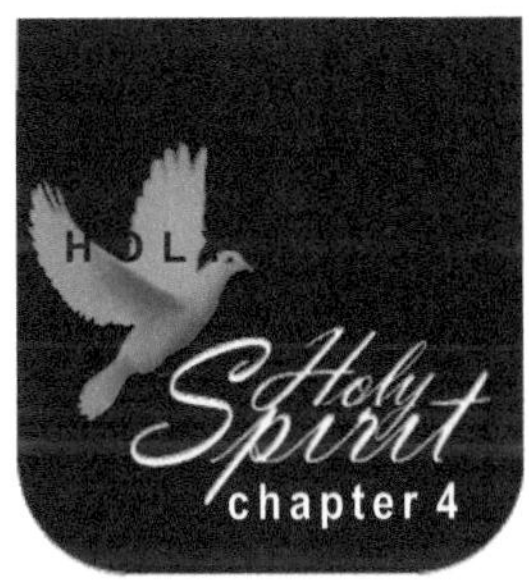

THE THREE KINDS OF SPIRIT

To truly know the worth and preciousness of the Holy Spirit of God, we need to examine the three spirits in the world. Lots of people only know about this physical and material world, but they failed to understand and have a proper grasp of the spiritual world. However, the fact remains that there is a spiritual world that largely determines what happens in the physical world. Man is essentially a spiritual being housed in a body, and these three spirits seek to control man one way or the other. Let's check them out:

a. **Human Spirit**

"The spirit of man is the candle of the LORD, searching all the inward parts of the belly." – Proverbs 20:27

"For what man knoweth the things of a man, save the spirit of man which is in him? even so the things of God knoweth no man, but the Spirit of God." – I Cor.

2:11

"Then shall the dust return to the earth as it was: and the spirit shall return unto God who gave it." – Ecclesiastes 12:7

The human spirit inhabits the body at conception and departs the physical body at the point of death. The human spirit is from God and it is what keeps man alive, though spiritually dead as a result of sin. The human spirit cannot relate with God unless it is regenerated at the point of conversion through the life-giving power of the Holy Spirit. The human spirit leads people into ungodliness, selfishness and dictates of the flesh. If it's regenerated, it will be greatly influenced by the Holy Spirit of God and if not, it will be possessed and dominated by the demonic spirit. Every human being has the human spirit keeping him alive till death.

> *You cannot live in isolation. Your spirit will either be controlled by the Spirit of life or the spirit of darkness.*

b.   **Demonic Spirit**

"And there was in their synagogue a man with an unclean spirit; and he cried out". – Mark 1:23

"For he said unto him, Come out of the man, thou unclean spirit. And he asked him, What is thy name? And he answered, saying, My name is Legion: for we are many." – Mark 5:8-9

The demonic spirits are fallen angels who rebelled with Satan. They are anti-human spirits that have the sole purpose of deceiving, dominating and destroying man. They seek to influence and control the spirit of man. They possess, oppress, dominate and rule the whole being of those who live in sin, wickedness and disobedience to God.

They bring sicknesses, diseases, torment, pains, fears and doubts to the body, soul and spirit of man, especially those that have not been regenerated. They bring darkness to the soul and alienate the spirit of man from God. They use the person, voice and being of a person through magic, idol worship, séances, transcended meditations and astral travels. Too many people in the world are being controlled by demonic spirits through their human spirits.

c. **Holy Spirit**

> **"Ye have not chosen me, but I have chosen you, and ordained you, that ye should go and bring forth fruit, and that your fruit should remain: that whatsoever ye shall ask of the Father in my name, he may give it you."** – John 15:16

> **"But the Comforter, which is the Holy Ghost, whom the Father will send in my name, he shall teach you all things, and bring all things to your remembrance, whatsoever I have said unto you."** – John 14:26

The Holy Spirit is the very Spirit of God. He enters into believers at regeneration in a measure and increases at baptism. A believer can be filled, saturated, drunk and drenched with the Spirit of God.

> **"And be not drunk with wine, wherein is excess; but be filled with the Spirit".** –
> Eph. 5:18.

If you are converted, the Holy Spirit will indwell your human spirit and produce the fruits of godliness in your life. The more you have the Holy Spirit, the more holy, godly and righteous you should be. If you give Him control of your life, He will never allow demonic spirits to come in, but when you repeatedly grieve, quench and vex Him, He will depart and the demonic spirits will take over your heart and life. It's either the Holy Spirit or demonic spirit influencing or controlling your human spirit. You cannot live in isolation. Your spirit will either be controlled by the Spirit of life or the spirit of darkness.

So, which spirit is possessing and controlling your heart and life? Which spirit have you yielded or covenanted your heart and life to? You cannot sit on the fence; you are either for God or you are for Satan. The fruits of your life so far show which spirit is dominating your human spirit. But you can yield your whole being to the Holy Spirit now, He is here for you.

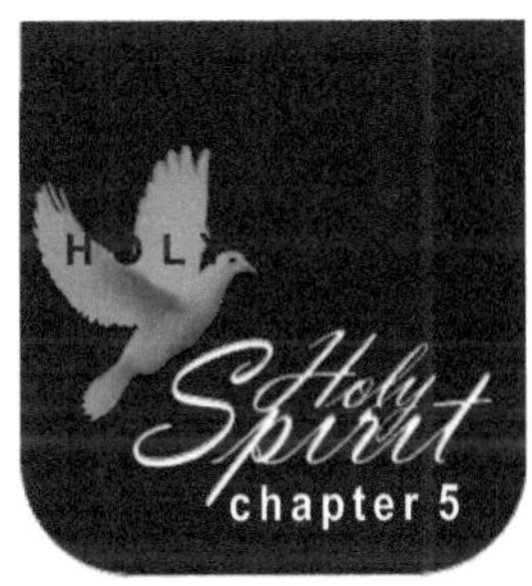

SPIRIT OF TRUTH
AND SPIRIT OF ERROR

" Even the Spirit of truth; whom the world cannot receive, because it seeth him not, neither knoweth him: but ye know him; for he dwelleth with you, and shall be in you." – John 14:17

The Holy Spirit of God is the Spirit of truth in all ramifications. He speaks the truth of God, in line with the word of God and the revealed mind of God. There is no lie, lying, deceit and twisting in the Spirit of the Lord. He is the Truth and the Spirit of Truth.

However, there is also the spirit of error that lies and twists the scriptures and deceive people to believe a lie.

"Now the Spirit speaketh expressly, that in the latter times some shall depart from the faith, giving heed to seducing spirits, and doctrines of devils;" – I

Timothy 4:1

These are demonic spirits that seduce people to teach doctrines of devils, but camouflage as truth. For example, a Pastor said; "God asked me to divorce my wife" - that is spirit of error. Another person said; "the spirit asked me to steal and misappropriate money" – that is seducing spirit. Some people give prophecies that provide occultic solutions and demonic way-outs to people, yet claiming that they are being led by the Spirit of God. Absolutely not! Rather they are being led by the spirit of error.

The Holy Spirit of God can never lead people against the word of God. The Holy Spirit as the Spirit of truth will never contradict the word of God. He will never give you a revelation, prophecy and special insight that go against the word of God. The word of God is greater and higher than any prophecy, dream, revelation and word of knowledge from any preacher or minister. The Holy Spirit will always defend and confirm the word of God, upholding the truth of God's word above everything else.

> *The word of God is greater and higher than any prophecy, dream, revelation and word of knowledge from any preacher or minister.*

But the spirit of error will always lift the word of God out of context, making it to mean what it is not and damn the souls of men. It is the spirit of error that makes preachers to preach gay living, support divorce, approve same-sex, teach pre-marital sex and teach that Christians can smoke, drink alcohol and approve the doctrine of eternal security which says that whatever you do after salvation doesn't matter.

Quite sad that many popular preachers that started with the Spirit of truth have gradually moved into the spirit of error today due to the false teachings they are now propounding; because of the secret sins they have failed to repent of. The Spirit of truth has left lots of preachers today and they are now teaching errors that damn them and their hearers in hell.

The love of money and things of this world have equally made many preachers to lose the Spirit of truth and embrace the spirit of error by which they now teach esoteric doctrines that contradict the revealed truth of God's infallible word. Yet, they will claim they are special revelations from God. What a tragedy!

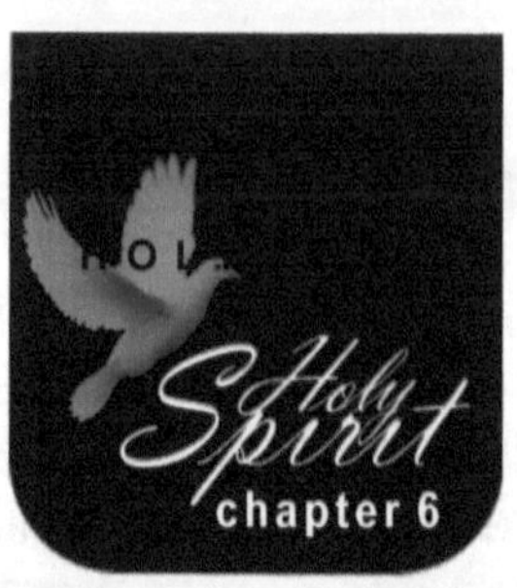

PURPOSE OF THE HOLY SPIRIT IN THE WORLD

In the creation of the world, the Holy Spirit was the One who incubated all that God later called into manifestation (Genesis 1:3). He is the One who was brooding over the surface of the earth just as the hen will brood over her eggs for 21 days before hatching. The Holy Spirit broods and incubates over the earth.

Throughout the Old Testament, the Father was in the forefront and the Son and the Spirit were in the background working with Him. During the earthly ministry of our Lord Jesus, the Lord Jesus was in the forefront, the Father and Holy Spirit were in the background. But since the Holy Spirit came down fully on the day of Pentecost (Acts 2:1-4), He has been here and have not gone back to heaven.

Surely, this is the age of the Holy Spirit. He is the One in charge now and His purpose of being here are:

1.   **To Be The Voice of God To The World:**
      The Holy Spirit is the One that takes the mind and

word of God and speaks them to us today. He is the One that makes us to understand what the Lord is saying to His people today. He communicates the voice of God to His church and people around the world.

2. **To Bring Sinners To Repentance:**
The Holy Spirit is here to bring people back to God. He is here to harvest souls for Christ, and He does that by bringing convictions of sin (John 6:7-11). He Redeems souls (John 3:3-5); Regenerates (Titus 3:5-7); Frees from sin (Romans 8:2); Changes lives (John 3:3-5);

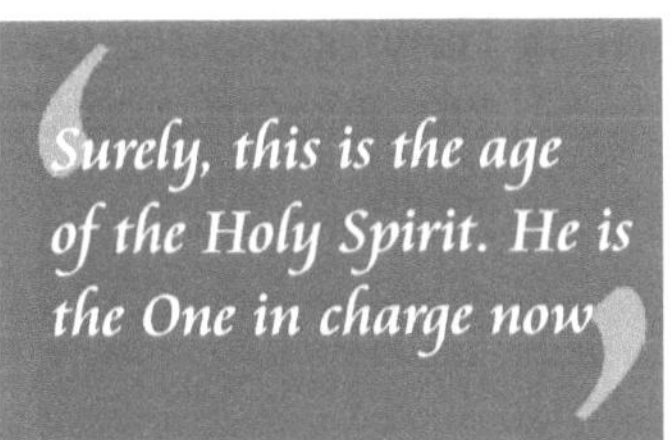

Washes sins away through the blood of Jesus (I Cor. 6:11) and bears witness with our spirit (John 15:26; Rom. 8:14-16).

3. **To Seal The Church Till The Day of Redemption:**
The Holy Spirit is here to perfect the church and keep her till the rapture. The Holy Spirit is here to guide the saints and glorify Christ in the church (Ephesians 1:13; 4:30).

4. **To Help Believers Live A Victorious Life:**
The Holy Spirit is here to help each and every believer to live a victorious life over sin, Satan and the systems of the world.

5. **He is Preventing The Anti-Christ:**
The Holy Spirit is the One hindering the anti-Christ from appearing (II Thess. 2:1-9). The anti-Christ is already in the world, with all the numbers, identity cards, associations and network of identities. But the Holy Spirit is here and the anti-Christ cannot appear as long as He is here. The Holy Spirit will continue to work until He will escort the saints to heaven during the rapture. That is why every believer must pray like the Psalmist; "Take not thy Holy Spirit from me" (Psalm 51:11). Without the Holy Spirit, no one can be taken up at rapture and whoever misses the rapture will be a sucker for the devil.

SATAN'S STRATEGIC WAR TO GET THE HOLY SPIRIT OUT OF THE CHURCH

❝So shall they fear the name of the LORD from the west, and his glory from the rising of the sun. When the enemy shall come in like a flood, the Spirit of the LORD shall lift up a standard against him". - Isaiah 59:19

The work of the Holy Spirit is diametrically opposed to that of Satan. While the Holy Spirit comes to give life, Satan comes to take life. While the Holy Spirit comes to save, restore and build, Satan comes to steal, kill and destroy. The Holy Spirit is in the world to lift up a standard against the works of the enemy. He is in the world to snatch as many souls as possible from the danger of hell. He reveals, thwarts, destroys and nullifies all the machinations and tricks of the devil to destroy the world, church, communities and individual lives.

Therefore, the devil hates the Holy Spirit with passion because he knew that He is here to foil and ruin all his plans against God and humanity, most especially the church of Christ. To get the church, the devil has strategically devised

---

ways to get the Holy Spirit out of the church, or at best, His presence and power will be minimal.

The Holy Spirit raised a young man not too long ago in Lagos. He was full of the presence and power of the Spirit of God and things began to happen. Crowd began to flock to his meetings and strong, accurate prophecies with attendant astounding miracles were the result. Amazing miracles were a daily occurrence and things were going great for some couple of years.

Then suddenly, the 'Prophet' announced to his bewildered audience that the Lord asked him to marry sixteen (16) wives. Though there were objections, but he went ahead and married sixteen women. Those who opposed it left the church and only very few people were left. This 'Prophet' was sure that he heard from the Lord. Few years later, the Holy Spirit sent another Prophet to him with a word of knowledge that what the Lord told him was that he should go and start 16 branches of his church, because 'the Church' is the wife of Christ, not to marry 16 women!

> *The Holy Spirit is in the world to lift up a standard against the works of the enemy.*

Unfortunately, the misinterpretation of what he heard allowed Satan to drive the Holy Spirit out of the church and in the life of that 'Prophet'. It is sad to note that too many churches that started so powerfully are in these scenarios today. Many who started with God have reverted to satanic worship and those who started with the Spirit of God have reverted to the flesh. This has now made the Holy Spirit to become a stranger in His church.

The devil will always use human reasoning such as secular, scientific and philosophical arguments to replace the Spirit of God in the church. He uses human liturgy, arrangements, false doctrines, dreams, revelations and misinterpretations of the scripture to make sure he whittles down the presence and power of the Holy Spirit.

Above all, he chooses his own agents to infiltrate churches and strategically get them into leadership positions in the church. Once they are there, they begin to run down the prayer life of the church; change the doctrines and de-emphasize the works of the Holy Spirit. Decisions will now be taken based on educational, humanistic theories and out goes the Holy Spirit from the church.

The section of the Catholic Church that welcomes and condones gay priests and those who sexually molest children are classical examples. The small sections of the congregational church of America, Episcopal and Anglicans of Great Britain are prime examples of the strategies of Satan to get the Holy Spirit out of the church through twisting of the scriptures to approve same sex marriage, gay living and making them priests. Once the Holy Spirit is out of the way, demonic, occultic and witchcraft spirits will be up and doing, damning many souls here and hereafter.

The big question every church leader must answer is this: How much of the presence of the Spirit of God has Satan successfully driven out of your church?

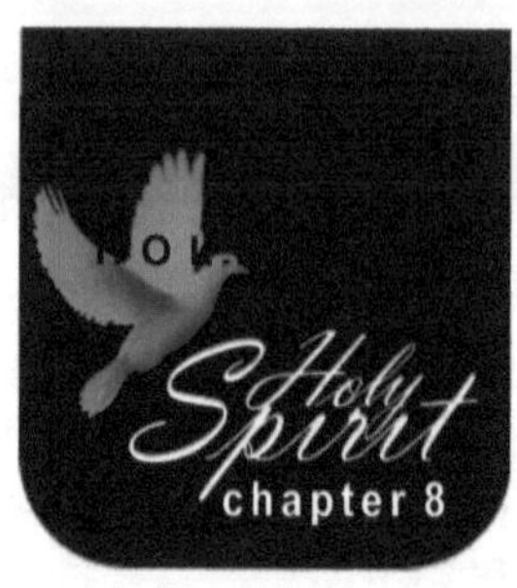

I WILL POUR OUT MY SPIRIT

"And it shall come to pass in the last days, saith God, I will pour out of my Spirit upon all flesh: and your sons and your daughters shall prophesy, and your young men shall see visions, and your old men shall dream dreams: And on my servants and on my handmaidens I will pour out in those days of my Spirit; and they shall prophesy:" – Acts 2:17-18.

Scripturally speaking, there are two principal prophecies for this end-time, which is the church age. The first prophecy talks about the people backsliding, being sinful, wicked and doing abominable things as the world grows worse and worse (I Timothy 4:1-2; II Timothy 3:1-5). The second prophecy talks about God pouring out His Spirit upon His people in that same last days (Acts 2:17-18). And both prophecies are being fulfilled simultaneously today.

While amazing apostasy, evil and wickedness are growing in the church and in the world, the Lord is also pouring out His Spirit like never before upon His people. You are the one that will choose which camp you will belong. While the devil is doing so much to take as many as possible to hell, God in His infinite mercy is also pouring out His Spirit and rescuing as many as are willing and preparing them for heaven.

Since the turn of the last 1900 century in Azusa Street in America, God has been pouring His Spirit with amazing manifestations of miracles, signs, wonders, healings and mighty harvest of souls. Records show that just over 80 years ago, Africa was less than 1 million professing Christians; but today through the mighty outpouring of the Holy Spirit in Nigeria, South Africa, Ivory Coast and Southern Africa, there are more than 400 million Christians.

> *While amazing apostasy, evil and wickedness are growing in the church and in the world, the Lord is also pouring out His Spirit like never before upon His people.*

A good example is the Baptist Church in Nigeria. Up till around Year 2000 they were still holding on to the doctrine of cessation of the Holy Spirit and His gifts. But when a new leader took over, he called for change and the doctrine was reviewed and the Baptist Churches welcomed the Person and gifts of the Holy Spirit back to their churches. Today, there is revival, life, vitality and growth of the Baptist Churches in Nigeria.

The Anglican Church in Nigeria is also on the same trail. Since they welcomed the presence and power of the Holy Spirit in the early nineties, the Anglican Communion has sprung back to life and growing in leaps and bounds with mighty miracles taking place.

All over the world today, God is pouring out His Holy Spirit and bringing people back to Him. The Holy Spirit is using dreams, revelations, healings and mighty demonstrations of His power to bring salvation in Jesus to people. China and Asia are good examples. Will you open up your heart and life to the Holy Spirit of God to be poured on you for revival? Will you allow yourself to be a great vessel in the hand of the Holy Spirit? His time is now!

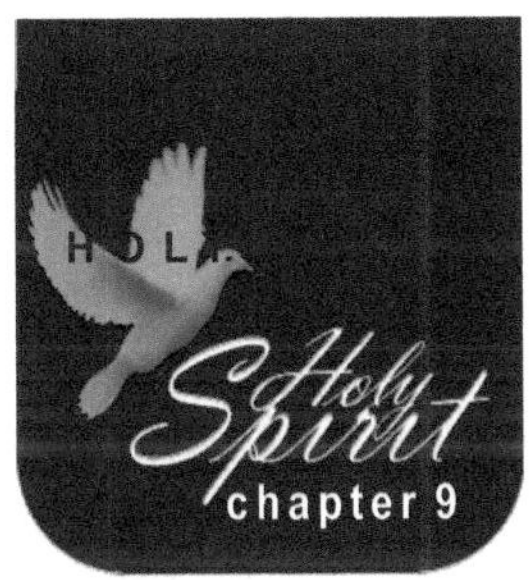

THE TRUE VICAR
OF THE CHURCH

A deeply spiritual man of God had a revelation in which he saw the devil preaching the gospel in a street corner. He was alarmed and asked the devil; "are you not the devil?" The devil answered; 'Yes'. "But why are you preaching the gospel of Christ then?" the man of God asked. The devil replied; "I have discovered that preaching the gospel without the presence and power of the Holy Spirit kills much more people than error". That is the position many churches have found themselves today because the power and presence of the Holy Spirit have been neglected in all things.

"Take heed therefore unto yourselves, and to all the flock, over the which the Holy Ghost hath made you overseers, to feed the church of God, which he hath purchased with his own blood." – Acts 20:28

One of the chief reasons why God sent His Holy Spirit into the world is because of the church, the body of Christ. The Holy

Spirit is to form, grow, guide, purge and glorify Christ in His church. The Holy Spirit is the genuine and true Overseer of the church. Our Lord Jesus has handed over the church into the hand and under the control of the Holy Spirit. He is to make the church what Christ intends her to be and prepare her ready for the rapture. The Holy Spirit is sent down from heaven and He's the power of the world to come.

> **"Unto whom it was revealed, that not unto themselves, but unto us they did minister the things, which are now reported unto you by them that have preached the gospel unto you with the Holy Ghost sent down from heaven; which things the angels desire to look into".** - 1 Peter 1:12.

* **The Holy Spirit directs where the gospel is to be preached and churches planted** – Acts 16:6-9.
He alone knows receptive hearts and where the field is ripe for harvest.

* **The Holy Spirit appoints men into offices of the Gospel work** – Acts 13:1-4.
He is the One that chooses, calls, commissions and qualifies men and women for various works in the vineyard of the Lord. And He is the one that chooses the field of operation for each person. He appoints and anoints for work in the house of the Lord.

* **The Holy Spirit forms the body of Christ in every locality** – I Cor. 12:13.
He is the One that brings Christians into the fellowship of the body of believers and gives life to

the assembly to be the true members of the body of Christ. He unites the believers in the body of Christ.

* **The Holy Spirit brings life, vitality, growth and health to the body of Christ.**
Individually and corporately, He works to bring warmth, life, spirituality, vitality, energy and divine infusion of grace to the church. No church can be alive without the living presence and power of the Holy Spirit.

* **The Holy Spirit transforms the believer into the image of Christ** – II Cor. 3:18; Gen. 1:2; Jude 20.
As we fellowship and commune with the Holy Spirit, He will transform every believer daily into the image of Christ. He forms Christ in every believer until we are Christ-like in every area of our lives.

* **The Holy Spirit Cleanses The Church** – Acts 5:10.
It is the work of the Holy Spirit to cleanse the church of every vestige of sin, corruption and ungodliness. He is the one perfecting the church and preparing her for the future. Without His work of cleansing and purging sins from the church, no church will be rapturable or fit to get to heaven. Therefore any church without the Holy Spirit is not a church. It's like a carousal going in circles with few riders, headed nowhere.

Without the Holy Spirit, there can be no church. Life, vitality, growth and dynamism are not possible without the presence and power of the Holy Spirit in the church. When a man is the vicar, controller and director of the church, then it is no longer the church of Christ, but a human organization with death and decay everywhere. When we use human philosophies, reasoning and academic excellence to drive the true Vicar away from His church, then it becomes a man-made religion, full of rituals but devoid of the life of God.

Many Pastors, church leaders and Christians are busy for the Lord without the full presence of the Holy Spirit in their lives, and the devil is happy with such situation. Living and life-giving churches are Holy Spirit churches. Growth and vitality will only come to churches that recognize the Holy Spirit and give Him preeminent control in the scheme of things.

> *Growth and vitality will only come to churches that recognize the Holy Spirit and give Him preeminent control in the scheme of things.*

One of the reasons for the spectacular growth of churches and mighty conversions today is the mighty workings of the Holy Spirit. Pentecostal churches who believe in the age, promise, person and gifts of the Holy Spirit are the fastest growing churches the world over today because they welcome the special presence of the Holy Spirit.

The presence and power of the Holy Spirit is non-negotiable if the church is to be virile and vibrant today. The Holy Spirit is the One that brings true growth and vitality (Acts 9:31); performs miracles and touches hearts for the Lord (John 3:3-5); He comforts, counsels and instructs believers (Acts 8:28; 13:2); He helps believers in prayers (Rom. 8:26-27); reminds, teaches and guides into all truth (John 14:16-26; 15:26); and reveals the deep things of God (I Cor. 2:9-12).

The first century church grew mightily because they gave preeminent position to the Holy Spirit (Acts 2:39; 5:32-33). Neglecting the Holy Spirit is signing the death warrant of the church. Dryness, lukewarmness, sins, formality and unspirituality of the church will be the order of the day when the door of the church is shut against the Holy Spirit. Living, liveliness and transformation will only be possible when the Holy Spirit is given unfettered access in our churches. Without the presence and power of the Holy Spirit, demons will have a field day in the church.

The Holy Spirit is the only power that can stop and conquer Satan in the world through the word of God, prayers, the name of Jesus and godly living. The church cannot make headway without the Holy Spirit. The disciples of Jesus learnt much under Him; they learnt theology, salvation, sanctification, prayer, church growth, evangelism, ethics, demonology, but all these were vain without the power of the Holy Spirit.

> **"And, behold, I send the promise of my Father upon you: but tarry ye in the city of Jerusalem, until ye be endued with power from on high."** – Luke 24:49.

The church can only begin to enjoy the presence and power of the Spirit today when we begin to recognize Him, love Him, fellowship with Him, praise Him and ask for His direction in all facets of our lives. We must make Him our Senior Partner and give Him preeminent position in the church. Then, things will happen!

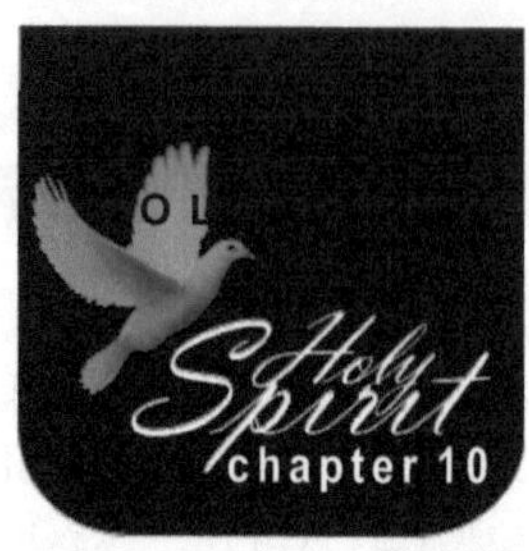

THE HOLY SPIRIT GLORIFIES AND TESTIFIES OF CHRIST

"This is he that came by water and blood, even Jesus Christ; not by water only, but by water and blood. And it is the Spirit that beareth witness, because the Spirit is truth. And there are three that bear witness in earth, the Spirit, and the water, and the blood: and these three agree in one". -1 John 5:6, 8;

"But when the Comforter is come, whom I will send unto you from the Father, even the Spirit of truth, which proceedeth from the Father, he shall testify of me:" -John 15:26;

"And we are his witnesses of these things; and so is also the Holy Ghost, whom God hath given to them that obey him". -Acts 5:32

One of the major reasons for the presence of the Holy Spirit in the world is to testify of Christ and glorify Him in the world. The Holy Spirit is to make sure that the work and sacrifice of Christ is not in vain in the world. The Holy Spirit elevates Christ and gives witness to the fact that Jesus Christ is the Lord.

Evangelist Reinhard Bonnke told the story of how he was invited to a town to conduct a meeting in an old church full of old people. There, he asked for the youths and the people replied that the youths are in the disco hall. He asked to be driven there in a car. Upon arrival, he met a hall full of young people, dancing and smoking away. He sought out the organizers and asked to speak for five minutes. Meanwhile, He was talking to the Holy Spirit to prove His presence.

Initially, they were noisy, but the Holy Spirit took over and at the end of his five minutes sermon, he left, but the dancing could not continue. They were arrested by the Holy Spirit and they all cried out to Jesus for forgiveness of sins and cleansing. By the time he returned to the city a year later, that disco hall had become a church and many of those young people are growing Christians. That is what the Holy Spirit does everyday, testifying of Christ and glorifying Him in the heart and life of men and women in the world.

The Holy Spirit is the most selfless Person I have ever known. He doesn't speak of Himself, but rather speaks of Christ.

It was the delight of the Son to glorify the Father; it is the delight of the Spirit to glorify the Son. Not that the Holy Spirit adds anything to the personal and mediatorial glories which now encircle Him as seated on the throne of His glory, but the Holy Spirit glorifies Jesus in the view and experience of men

> **"Howbeit when he, the Spirit of truth, is come, he will guide you into all truth: for he shall not speak of himself; but whatsoever he shall hear, that shall he speak: and he will shew you things to come. He shall glorify me: for he shall receive of mine, and shall shew it unto you. All things that the Father hath are mine: therefore said I, that he shall take of mine, and shall shew it unto you."** -John 16:13-15.

Indeed, it is truly delightful to notice the different instances of glorifying that we have here. The Son glorifies the Father on earth; the Father glorifies the Son in heaven. And now again the Holy Spirit glorifies Christ on earth, in the hearts and lives of His people.

The Holy Spirit is the most selfless Person I have ever known. He doesn't speak of Himself, but rather speaks of Christ. He elevates, honours and glorifies Christ. He is most tireless; always working to bring men to Christ and edify the saints. He is the most powerful to save, heal, deliver and destroy all the works of the devil. He is the most persistent and undiscouraged Person I have ever known. Even, when believers fall into sin, He will work to bring restoration and gently woo the sinner to come to Christ in spite of repeated rebuff and rejections.

The Holy Spirit is truly an amazing Person that does everything to testify and glorify Christ. Though we don't recognize Him, yet He keeps working to bring our hearts and lives back to Christ. Shouldn't we then appreciate and allow such an amazing Person in our hearts to drive out any unChrist-likeness from us?

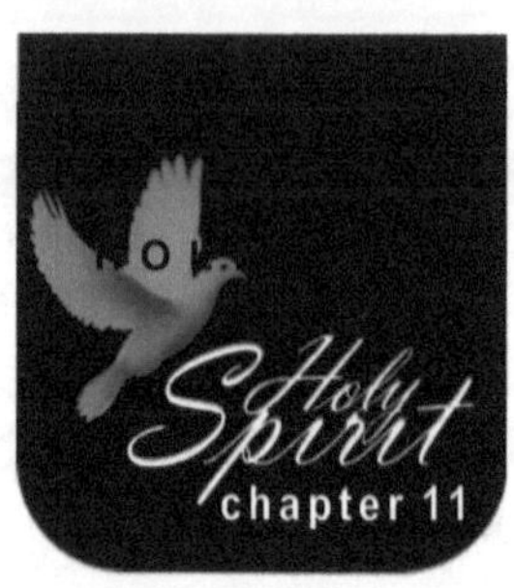

BAPTISM WITH THE HOLY SPIRIT

The baptism of the Holy Spirit is of great essence in our Christian life. In my own experience over the years, I can attest to the fact that victorious Christian living over sin, Satan and sicknesses will be nearly impossible without the baptism or infilling of the Holy Spirit. I did not get baptized in the Holy Spirit immediately. I got born again in January 1982 and it took me almost a year to get baptized. This was due largely to my unbelief, doubt and little hunger for the experience. But when I became hungry enough, I got baptized in the Holy Spirit in a meeting held some days later in our church then.

I knew the Holy Spirit filled me and a strange tongue welled up within me. The first thing I noticed is that my prayer life took a turn for the better. Before, it was a struggle to pray, read the Bible and live victoriously, but after the baptism of the Holy Spirit, I found out that I could pray for hours, live victoriously and even have power to pray for people to be healed and delivered of demons!

The word 'Baptizo' is the Greek word that means – to be submerged, dipped under, filled, saturated, drunk and drenched. To be baptized with the Holy Spirit then means that one is possessed, filled, saturated and arrayed with God's Spirit and power (Acts 1:4-5).

> **"I indeed baptize you with water unto repentance: but he that cometh after me is mightier than I, whose shoes I am not worthy to bear: he shall baptize you with the Holy Ghost, and with fire:"** - Matthew 3:11.

It is a definite experience that every Christian must have after salvation. Jesus asked His disciples to wait for it and every born again Christian must seek God to be baptized in the Holy Spirit. Without it, no one can truly live a dynamic, powerful, victorious and prevailing Christian life.

The Baptism of the Holy Spirit is not known to the Old Testament saints. The Spirit only comes upon them for special service and after the service He would leave them, with the exception of some good ones. For instance; Balaam (Numbers 24:2); Samson (Judges 13:24-25); Othniel (Judges 3:10); Gideon (Judges 6:34) and Saul (1 Sam. 10:6-13).

It is a definite experience that every Christian must have after salvation.

The exceptions are Joseph (Gen. 41:31-39); Joshua (Numbers 27:18); Daniel (Dan. 4:8-9, 18; 5:11-14). A special case is in the construction and furnishing of the Tabernacle in the wilderness. God specially filled Bezaleel with His Spirit so that he can wrought great works (Exod.

31:1-11) and so did God to all the prophets (2 Pet. 1:21).

This is the great demerit of the Old Testament saints; they did not have the spirit within them, only upon them. That is why they were not able to obey God and live victoriously over sin. The Lord saw this and promised a new covenant whereby the Holy Spirit will reside inside us and be teaching us to obey God and live for Him (Ezekiel 36:26-28).

Clarifying the Baptism of the Holy Spirit:
At salvation, every believer has the Spirit in a measure. Every born again Christian has the Holy Spirit at salvation, because it is the Spirit that quickens you to life as you repent genuinely and gives you a witness that you have been forgiven and saved (Rom. 8:14-16). After salvation, you may be baptized into the body of Christ and do water baptism, yet you are not yet baptized with the Holy Spirit.

The Christian life begins at Calvary, but the Christian service begins at Pentecost. At salvation, we are imparted with divine life, but at Holy Spirit baptism, we get impartation of power for service. At salvation, we have the Holy Spirit as a 'resident', but at baptism, we have Him as 'president'. At salvation, we have Him in a small measure, but it is at the baptism of the Holy Spirit that the believer can be Spirit-filled, controlled, power-packed and dynamic. Baptism to the body of Christ which we experience at salvation is the work of the Spirit of God, but baptism with the Holy Spirit is a promise by Jesus Christ. (Matt. 3:11; John 7:37-39).

Jesus is the Baptizer in the Holy Spirit:
The baptism of the Holy Spirit is a gift from God to His church so that she might be effective. Baptism in the Holy Spirit was prophesied in the Old Testament for this church age (Joel 2:28-29; Acts 2:17-18, 39). John the Baptist

preached it (Matt. 3:11; Luke 3:16; John 1:30-34). This is surely a new experience for every new believer.

The Old Testament saints never knew of this experience but was kept for the believers in Christ (Heb. 8:6; 11:39-40). Jesus promised it to the believers (John 7:37-39; Luke 24:49; Acts 1:4-8; Luke 11:9:13). Jesus specifically instructed the disciples to wait for the promise of the Father and they waited and were baptized in the Holy Spirit on the day of Pentecost (Acts 2:1-4).

The baptism of the Holy Spirit will make Him to be our 'Parakletos' – a helper alongside. He will be all that Jesus will be to us. He will be living inside of us and help us in every possible way to live for Christ and be effective for God in the world (John 14:16-18).

The Holy Spirit baptism is a definite experience (Acts 19:1-6).
You will know whether you have received it or not. The initial evidence of being baptized with the Holy Spirit is speaking in an unknown, unlearned language. In the scripture, believers at Pentecost (Acts 2:1-4); Cornelius and his colleagues (Acts 10:44-45) and believers at Ephesus (Acts 19:1-6) all spoke in tongues when they were baptized with the Holy Spirit.

I have found that to be true in my experience also. I have had cause to lay hands on many people and they spoke in unlearned, heavenly tongue. However, this is an initial evidence; it must be developed and cultured. By engaging in constant communion, prayers, fasting and fellowship with the Holy Spirit, you will begin to flow in His power, gifts and anointing.

To be baptized with the Holy Spirit is conditional. If you are not genuinely born again, saved from sins, sanctified, holy within and without, you cannot be filled with the Spirit of God. He is a Holy Spirit, He will not come and dwell in a heart filled with hatred, bitterness, lust, stubbornness, disobedience and unforgiving spirit. You must purge yourself of all these, then hunger and thirst for Him, determine to obey God in every area of your life and pray persistently in faith (Mark 11:22-24).

> *You cannot live in power, nor be a threat to the kingdom of darkness without the baptism of the Holy Spirit.*

You cannot live in power, nor be a threat to the kingdom of darkness without the baptism of the Holy Spirit. You will always be living a defeated, nominal, powerless and lukewarm life when you have not been baptized in the Holy Spirit.

"Then Peter said unto them, Repent and be baptized every one of you in the name of Jesus Christ for the remission of sins and ye shall receive the gift of the Holy Ghost. For the promise is unto you, and to your children, and to all that are afar off, even as many as the Lord our God shall call". – Acts 2:38-39.

This promise is unto you, so what are you waiting for?

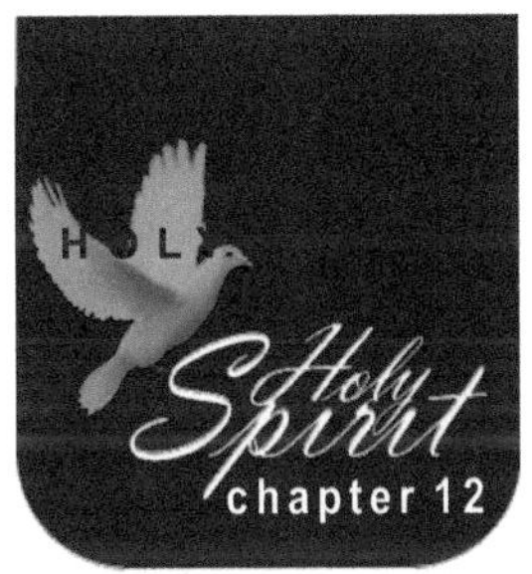

SPEAKING IN TONGUES

❝ But ye, beloved, building up yourselves on your most holy faith, praying in the Holy Ghost" -Jude 20.

Yes, speaking in tongues have been largely bastardized today. Firstly, some theologians who interpret the Bible with their secular mindsets have written against it as 'gassollalia' – gibberish; they say it is worthless. The devil is aware of its importance and he tries to prevent the believer from this blessed experience by the objection to its veracity by many respected theologians. Many of them are claiming that we no longer need it today and that it is not scriptural. However, nothing could be farther from the truth.

Secondly, there are learned tongues today. Some people who cannot meet the scriptural conditions of being baptized with the Holy Spirit of God have gone ahead to have a school where they teach people to speak in tongues! I have heard some people speak in learned tongues in some meeting. Even some Christians, who wanted to show off to others that they too have been baptized in the Holy Spirit, whereas they are not, speak in configured or manufactured tongues which are definitely not from the Spirit of God.

Thirdly, there are terrestrial and celestial tongues. Lots of demonized, occultic and Satan inspired tongues abound in the body of Christ today. Lots of preachers and Christian workers who claim to be speaking in tongues are living waywardly. Witches, wizards and familiar spirits are also speaking in tongues in the church just to deceive the uninformed. Speaking in tongues with immoral, disobedient and carnal lifestyles is incompatible with scripture.

Be that as it may, there is Holy Spirit inspired, heavenly tongues today. Speaking in tongues as an initial evidence of being baptized in the Spirit is foundational. You must pick up from there to move into deeper fellowship with the Holy Spirit by practicing and using this God-given prayer language everyday. (Luke 1:35).

> **"And the earth was without form, and void; and darkness was upon the face of the deep. And the Spirit of God moved upon the face of the waters"**. - Genesis 1:2.

> **"The grace of the Lord Jesus Christ, and the love of God, and the communion of the Holy Ghost, be with you all. Amen."** - II Cor. 13:14.

> **"But ye, beloved, building up yourselves on your most holy faith, praying in the Holy Ghost"** -Jude 20.

By praying in your prayer language, you are being overshadowed and incubated by the Spirit of God. And that will produce the fruits of the Spirit and godliness in your life. The Lord did not give any useless thing to His people. Tongues are the highway of communion with God. The more you pray in tongues, the more you flow in the Spirit; the more you have deep insight into the things of God. Both the Bible and experience have shown that the more we speak in Holy Spirit inspired tongues, the more we prevail with God, build up ourselves, Christ's character being formed in us, gifts of the Spirit being manifested more in our lives and more intimate presence of God being enjoyed.

Speaking in tongues as an initial evidence of being baptized in the Spirit is foundational.

"For he that speaketh in an unknown tongue speaketh not unto men, but unto God: for no man understandeth him; howbeit in the spirit he speaketh mysteries. He that speaketh in an unknown tongue edifieth himself; but he that prophesieth edifieth the church". – I Cor. 14:2, 4.

Praying in tongues helps me to pray for needs through the Spirit. There are occasions that I need to pray for people and I don't know what to pray for, I just switch over to my prayer language, and sooner or later, the result will come. At the baptism of the Holy Spirit, you have the Spirit and power baptism (Acts 10:38), but the power will only begin to flow after you have been able to separate time to fast and pray in tongues.

Tongues are not for showmanship as some Charismatic believers are doing today, but a means of deep communion with the Lord. Tongues help us to pray in the Spirit and allow the Spirit to pray through us. When you take time to do protracted fasting and praying in tongues, you will experience a lot of power demonstration and manifestations of the gifts of the Spirit. If you want to understand, speak and walk in spiritual mysteries of God, then learn to use tongues in your private prayers. Let the Spirit pray, groan and intercede through you.

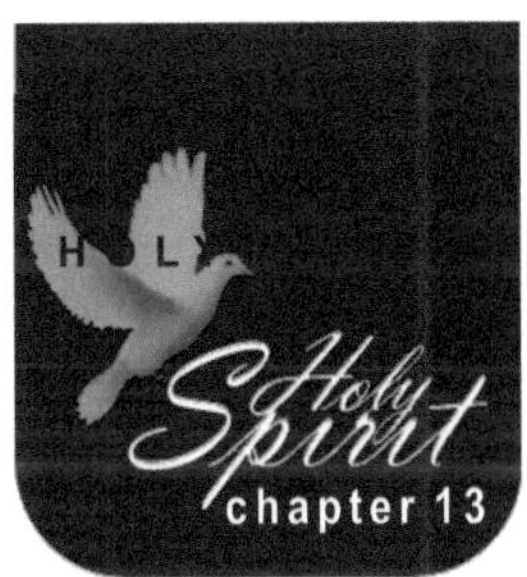

HOLY SPIRIT IN THE LIFE AND MINISTRY OF OUR LORD JESUS CHRIST

God the Father is distinct and personal, so also God the Son and God the Spirit, yet the three are one. The Father is not the Son, the Son is not the Spirit and yet are one and inseparable. The Holy Spirit was prominent in the earthly life of Christ. He lived, taught, worked, conquered sin and won victories for God in the same Spirit whom we may have today. The same Spirit that helped Him in His earthly life is ever ready to help us today. In the incarnation of Christ, He was total man and total God. However, He suspended His divine attributes while he was here and did not use it for a single day.

> **"Let this mind be in you, which was also in Christ Jesus: Who, being in the form of God, thought it not robbery to be equal with God: But made himself of no reputation, and took upon him the form of a servant, and was made in the likeness of men:"** – Phil. 2:5-7.

"But of that day and hour knoweth no man, no, not angels of heaven, but my Father only". - Matt. 24:36.

That is why He was sometimes wearied, tired, slept and answered that He did not know the exact time the world will end. If He had not suspended His divine attributes while here, He would obviously have known. By suspending His divine attributes while here to die for sinners, He would therefore have to depend on the Holy Spirit for all He would accomplish here. The following will confirm the work of the Holy Spirit in the life and ministry of the Lord Jesus:

i.   **Jesus Christ was begotten of the Holy Spirit** – Luke 1:35; Matt. 1:18, 20. Jesus can be rightly called the 'Son of the Holy Spirit' because it was the Spirit of God that overshadowed Mary until she was pregnant with the baby Jesus without human contribution. The Holy Spirit was the agent of the Father in the incarnation of the Son. If the overshadowing of the Holy Spirit produced Christ through Mary, how we need Him to produce Christ in us today!

ii.   **Christ was prophesied by the Holy Spirit** – Heb. 10:7; Luke 24:26-27; John 5:39.

iii.   **He was anointed by the Holy Spirit** – Matt. 3:13-17; Luke 3:21-22; 4:1, 14. In actual fact Christ never started His earthly ministry without the baptism and presence of the Holy Spirit in His life. He waited to be baptized in the Spirit before commencing His atoning ministry. What a lesson to us ministers today!

Christ was led by the Spirit (Matt. 4:1; Luke 4); Baptized by the Spirit (Matt. 3:16; Luke 4:1); Filled with the Spirit (John 1:33; 3:34); Had the Spirit in measureless fullness (John 3:34); He spoke by the power of the Spirit (John 6:63; Isaiah 11:2); He performed His miracles by the power of the Spirit (Acts 10:38; Luke 4:18; Matt. 12:28); He offered Himself to die for sinners by the Spirit (Heb. 9:14); He was resurrected by the Spirit (Rom. 8:11) and He gave commands to the disciples by the Spirit (Acts 1:2).

It is now evidently clear that all that Jesus did was through the power of the Holy Spirit. He lived, prayed, worked and conquered the power of demons and Satan triumphantly through the power of the Holy Spirit. The same dynamic person and power of the Holy Spirit is at our disposal for service and conflict with Satan and sins. Through the same Spirit, we can offer ourselves to God without spot or wrinkle as the Lord did.

> *If the Lord was anointed for service, we too must be anointed.*

"How much more shall the blood of Christ, who through the eternal Spirit offered himself without spot to God, purge your conscience from dead works to serve the living God?" – Heb. 9:14.

If the Lord was anointed for service, we too must be anointed. The same Spirit that enabled the Lord to do great exploits is still available with His power today if we will recognize, love, cherish, adhere and fellowship with Him.

Whoever makes himself a clean and pure vessel will be used by the Holy Spirit to cause mighty revolutions in the lives of the people today. Though, our Lord Jesus received the Holy Spirit in measureless fullness, ours is in a measure. Yet, we can be filled again and again until we are drunk with the Spirit and amazing things will begin to happen through us and by us.

> **"And be not drunk with wine, wherein is excess; but be filled with the Spirit".** –
> Eph. 5:18.

HOLY SPIRIT IN THE LIFE AND MINISTRY OF THE APOSTLES

The Apostles of Christ deeply recognized the Holy Spirit. They took Him as the true representative of Jesus and gave Him preeminent place in their lives and work. The Book of Acts is truly the acts of the Holy Spirit simply because the Apostles did not use or manipulate the Holy Spirit according to their whims and caprices, but they allowed Him to operate and simply followed His biddings and instructions. They recognized His leadership and followed His instructions. Check out these steps:

1. **They waited for the Holy Spirit** – Acts 2:1-4.
    We must take time to seek His presence, wait upon Him, and spend time in prayers and fasting until He fills us with His power and gifts. He will do in a day what we cannot do in 100 years. Jumping into God's work without the clear presence and power of the Holy Spirit is a treatise to disaster. Wait on the Lord until you are clothed with power, then you can go forth to reap the harvest.

2. **They constantly seek His re-filling** – Acts 4:31; Rev. 1:10; Eph. 5:18.

They were never satisfied. They constantly sought for more infilling of the Spirit. They knew that once is never enough. It is important to be filled again and again with the Spirit. Activities, labours, talking and commitments do leak the Spirit away from our lives, so we need to go back to be renewed, filled and drenched again and again.

3. **They prayed in the power of the Holy Spirit** – Rom. 8:26; Acts 4:23-31.

The Apostles asked for His leading and recognized Him as their Senior prayer leader. They prayed in the Spirit, prayed His prayer points, and thereby never experienced unanswered prayers. Until we allow Him to be our Senior prayer leader and ready to obey His prayer promptings, we shall be powerless in our prayers. When our prayer points are from men and their prayer point books, then we relegate the Holy Spirit to the background. The Holy Spirit has prayer points for every occasion and situation and when you pray His prayers; your answers will be outstanding.

4. **They welcomed His gifts** – Acts 2:17-18; 8:1-17; I Tim. 4:14; Rom. 1:11.

The Apostles gave room to the gifts and operations of the Holy Spirit in their services. They welcomed His voice in dreams, visions, and revelations. They did not quench His ministrations. The manifestations of the gifts of the Holy Spirit must never be subdued in our churches. Once we form the habit of subduing and rejecting His gifts and manifestations, then He will quietly withdraw and everything will become empty and lifeless.

5. **They followed His leading in the field of evangelism** – Acts 13:1-4; 16:6-7; 8:29, 39
    The Apostles allowed and welcomed the leading of the Holy Spirit. They only went to wherever He led and appointed only those whom He appointed. They sought His leading on where to preach and thereby recorded amazing breakthroughs. The Holy Spirit is the Lord of the harvest and if we take time to seek His leading, our gospel witness cannot be fruitless. If we obey and choose whom He chooses, the work cannot but be fruitful and growing.

    > *Until we allow Him to be our Senior prayer leader and ready to obey His prayer promptings, we shall be powerless in our prayers.*

6. **They accorded Him pre-eminent position** – Acts 6:3; 19:1-6; 5:32.
    The Apostles made being filled with the Spirit the qualification for His usage. They preached and emphasized His baptism and want everyone to be possessed with Him. Nobody should be a worker in the church who is not filled with the Holy Spirit.

7. **They spoke by His power and performed miracles** – Acts 1:8; 6:5-10; 5:33.
    They were aware that without His power, they are powerless. They therefore sought His power and He performed the miraculous through them. The Bible is the 'sword of the Spirit' (Eph. 6:17). The word alone

is not enough. Truth without the power of the Spirit will deaden as much as error. We need the Spirit to quicken the word (II Cor. 3:3-6). Our prayer is to be filled by the Spirit in order to be effective (Jude 20). So everything boils down to the Holy Spirit. Without His presence and power in our lives, supernatural ministry is impossible.

8. **They taught by His progressive revelations** – I Cor. 2:9-11; John 16:13; Acts 15:2

It was the Sprit that revealed and taught them all those truths they propounded which were in line with the Old Testament and showed the mind of God in greater dimension. They sought His mind and heart in matters of doctrine and life. It is not possible to escape error and damnable doctrines that drown men in perdition without the Holy Spirit of God. Men that started well but deviated into erroneous teachings and special revelations that negate the uniform doctrines of the scripture have long lost their step with the Holy Spirit of God.

9. **He confirmed their witness and prospered the work in their hands** – Acts 5:12-16; 11:12; Mark 16:20.

Without the mighty workings of the Holy Spirit in our lives and ministry, the work will be hard and fruitless. It was the Holy Spirit that actually did the work through the Apostles and performed all the miracles, signs and wonders. We cannot change anybody, but we can be the vessel through whom the Holy Spirit can flow to bring changes to the lives, families and destinies of people we come in contact with. Therefore, we cannot succeed without Him. The more earnest we seek Him, the better for our lives and work.

10. **He cleansed the church when they allowed His unhindered move** – Acts 5:1-10.
The Holy Spirit kept and cleansed the first century church because the Apostles allowed Him to move unhindered and unfettered. He purged the church of sins and dealt with the rebellious and hypocrites. How we desperately need the same cleansing and purging from sins and evils in the church of this end time. But where are the leader that will allow the Holy Spirit to work in their lives and church without let or hindrance?

Because the Apostles welcomed, recognized, allowed, accepted and fellowshipped with the Holy Spirit and made Him their Senior life and ministry partner (Acts 15:28) they experienced great things, such as; Great power and grace (Acts 4:33); Great fear upon the people (Acts 5:11); Great wonders and miracles (Acts 6:8); Great persecution (Acts 8:1); Great suffering (Acts 9:16) and Great joy and growth (Acts 8:8-9).

As Christians and ministers of these last days, we cannot but follow the worthy examples of the first Apostles if we are to experience great things in our lives and ministries today. The Holy Spirit has not diminished in His power and desire to save, heal, harvest souls to the King and glorify Christ on earth.

The trouble today is that majority of us have the mentality that the Holy Spirit is just an experience or a force, not a person that was sent here to help us. It's time to change that mentality and recognize the person and presence of the Holy Spirit anew. We must give Him the pre-eminent control and allow Him to work and take the lead. If you and I are able to do that to a great degree, then the days of the acts of Apostles are here again.

THE PRESENCE AND POWER OF THE HOLY SPIRIT

"And he said, My presence shall go with thee, and I will give thee rest. And he said unto him, If thy presence go not with me, carry us not up hence". - Exodus 33:14-15.

It is the presence and power of the Holy Spirit in our lives and churches that will make the mighty difference. A preacher was invited to preach in a foreign country. He prepared very well, prayed and honoured the invitation. While seated in the service and waiting to be introduced, the Holy Spirit whispered to him to change his message. He was told by the Spirit of the Lord to jettison his favourite message and rather preach on salvation of souls.

After the initial struggle, he obeyed and spoke powerfully on the need for everyone to get saved and have personal relationship with God. He gave an altar call and the whole church, including the Senior Pastor came out to receive Christ! The presence and power of the Holy Spirit made the difference in the church that day.

Moses knew this truth and cried to the Lord that His presence must go with them in the wilderness journey. In looking at the presence and power of the Holy Spirit in the church, we can see three types of presence:

a.   **The Omnipresence of God**:
God the Spirit is everywhere at the same time. The Psalmist says in Psalm 139:7-10;

> **"Whither shall I go from thy spirit? or whither shall I flee from thy presence? If I ascend up to heaven, thou art there: if I make my bed in hell, behold, thou art there. If I take the wings of the morning, and dwell in the uttermost parts of the sea; Even there shall thy hand lead me and thy right hand shall hold me."**

The Omnipresence of God knows everywhere, everything and at the same time. He sees what's going on and nothing can be hidden from Him. He is present at every room, house, street, community and nation every time, though many don't know, nor see Him.

b.   **The Indwelling Presence of God**
Once you are born again and baptized in the Holy Spirit, He is inside you. Every genuine believer is indwelt by the Spirit of the living God.

> **"Ye are of God, little children, and have overcome them: because greater is he**

that is in you, than he that is in the world". - I John 4:4.

"For as many as are led by the Spirit of God, they are the sons of God". -Rom. 8:14.

"And I will pray the Father, and he shall give you another Comforter, that he may abide with you for ever; Even the Spirit of truth; whom the world cannot receive, because it seeth him not, neither knoweth him: but ye know him; for he dweleth with you, and shall be in you. Jesus answered and said unto him, If a man love me, he will keep my words: and my Father will love him, and we will come unto him, and make our abode with him". -John 14:16-17, 23.

The Father, Son and the Holy Spirit will indwell the believer; so long he is clean, pure, and holy in heart and life. His indwelling will give him inner strength and rivers of living waters will flow out of him. His indwelling presence will make life, power and rivers of spiritual blessings to flow out of a believer to others. That is why it's always important to be filled and drunk with the Spirit.

> *It is His presence that will bring presents to those who are presently present in His presence.*

c.		**The Manifest Presence of God** – Psalm 114:1-7. This is the physical, revealed and manifest demonstration of

His power and glory. This is Shekinah glory manifesting to remove barriers, obstacles, perform signs, wonders and amazing power demonstrations to heal, save, deliver and bring turn around to people, churches and groups. The manifest presence of the Holy Spirit will result in defeat to the enemy, supernatural demonstrations of His gifts, power for miracles and mighty impact.

It is His manifest presence that must be our heart and hard cry. And it takes times of communion with Him, fasting, self-denials, practicing His presence, pure motives and not sharing His glory to see His manifest and Shekinah glory in our lives and churches. It is His presence that will bring presents to those who are presently present in His presence. His manifest presence must be high, great, constant and consuming in the church if things will work.

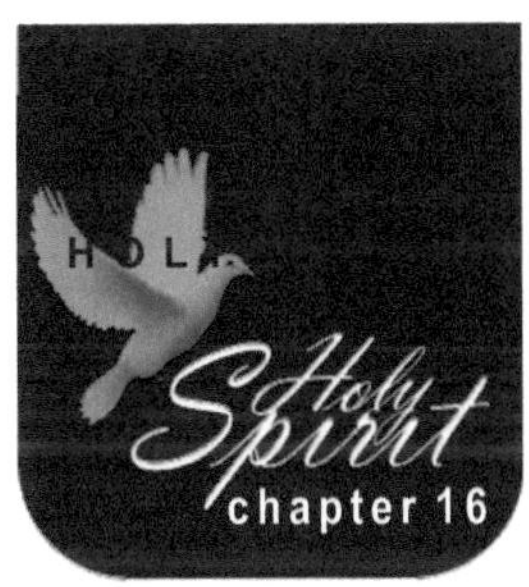

COMMUNION WITH THE HOLY SPIRIT

❝The grace of the Lord Jesus Christ, and the love of God, and the communion of the Holy Ghost, be with you all. Amen.❞ -II Cor. 13:14.

If we are really going to see and experience the Shekinah presence of the blessed Holy Spirit in our personal lives and churches, then we must start to practice communion with Him afresh. Communion is not only what we read during the benediction to a service, but a practical recognition of the Holy Spirit as a divine person and taking ample time to commune with Him daily.

Since I learnt this truth, I have enjoyed untold benefits. How else could I have written this book without the communion of the Holy Spirit? By communing with the Spirit of life, He led me to marry my wife over 23 years ago. He led me during my pastoral ministry with amazing miracles, growth and transformation of lives as a result. He led me into the Church Growth Ministry by orchestrating my timely resignation, securing my first office and starting the seminars, school and trainings gradually since 1994. And He still leads me to which topic or issues to address in each of our conferences and which books to write. It has taken me 25 years to write this book because it is now He releases me to write it, though it has been inside of me that long years.

Looking at the word; 'Communion', it means eleven (11) things the Holy Spirit wants to do or will do for any leader or church. Taking time to commune with Him in deep prayers, fasting, holy living, studying of the scriptures and praying in your spiritual prayer language will bring His presence to do these eleven things for you:

1. **Partnership**
    As you commune with the Spirit of God, He becomes your partner in life and ministry. As your Senior Partner, He will lead, guide, guard and direct you to the right place of fruitfulness in ministry. He will partner with you to do effective and impactful work for the Lord. The Holy Spirit cannot be your partner and your ministry will be barren. The Holy Spirit cannot be your Senior Partner and you are still confused in ministry.

2. **Fellowship**
    Your communion with Him will make Him have deep fellowship with you and therefore can reveal the secret things of the Lord to you. He will speak to you in a way you will understand. He will not leave you in the dark concerning anything you need or want to know. Deep fellowship with Him will make Him to open up your life before you and open up any hidden sin, facts and things you need to know that have

been hindrances to your life, work and destiny.

3.   Distributorship

The Holy Spirit will become your distributor. He will go to the presence of God, take the blessings you need and come and distribute them to your life and church. He is the One allowed to get the presence of God on your behalf to bring things down for you. He takes the heart, mind, words and thoughts of God

> *Communion brings the power of the Holy Spirit into practical display in your life and church.*

from His throne and relay them to us in the way we will understand and until we respond obediently. He is the true distributor of God's grace, power and mercy to His people.

4.   Helper

Communion with the Holy Spirit turns Him to our helper. He helps and enables us to live right, take right decisions and to stand for what is right in the face of persecutions and adversity. The Holy Spirit helps our infirmities and helps us to overcome the flesh. He is the present help in times of trouble.

5.   Empowerer

Communion brings the power of the Holy Spirit into practical display in your life and church. He will empower you to work, serve and back up the word of God in your mouth and life. You will go in His power and your ministry will be in the days of His power. He will empower you to work in His might.

6. **Intercessor**

The Holy Spirit is the greatest intercessor. He will pray with you and pray for you with intensity and spiritual fervency. Many times we cannot pray as we should, yet He will come to pray through you and help you to pray in the right way and for the right requests.

7. **Strengthener**

He strengthens us with divine strength. He gives the strength to run without fainting and walk without being weary. He will strengthen you physically, spiritually, mentally, ministerially and financially. His will strengthen you with the strength of God to do the impossible.

8. **Nourisher**

The Holy Spirit nourishes the body, soul and spirit of the believer. He feeds us with the appropriate food that will help our spiritual growth and consistent walk with the Lord. He nourishes us through challenges, trials, learning process and practical learning of the mercy, favour and goodness of the Lord. He will never leave your soul famished if you truly commune regularly with Him. He will always fill you with the fullness of God.

9. **Protector**

He protects and preserves us from the fiery darts and attacks of the enemy. Many times He will ward off the arrows of the wicked and lift up a standard against the flood of the wicked and ungodly men. He protects our heart and spirit from the onslaught of evil thoughts and words of men and demonic activities. Sometimes, He reveals the wicked plots of the enemy to us, but many times He destroys them without even showing them to us. What a mighty protector we have!

10. **Sustainer**

The Holy Spirit seals and sustains the saints till the day of death or rapture. He is the seal of God in the life of every believer. And as long as we commune with Him, the seal remains sacrosanct in our lives. He keeps the feet of His saints and does not want His labour to be in vain over any believer.

11. **Comforter and Counselor**

He brings comfort, consolation, joy and peaceful counsel of the Lord to our heart and life. He brings order out of every chaos and sweetens the soul of those who know Him.

It's time we call the whole body of believers into whole days of communion with the Holy Spirit like never before. In communion with Him, we leave the direction and leadership in His hands. He knows what to pray for in our lives and churches: it is then we can enjoy these untold benefits. If our lives are beggarly, shallow and powerless, it is because we have chosen to ignore deep fellowship and communion with the Spirit of life.

I make bold to say that it is deep communion with the Holy Spirit that gave birth to this book. All these years that I have the mind to write this book, I didn't know until one morning that I received grace to really pray in a hotel room, while ministering for a pastor at Ibadan, Oyo State, Nigeria. It was in that prayer that I received the outline, topics and layout of this book. I quickly took my note and wrote everything down. After that, I knew the book is already done. All because I had a deep communion with the Holy Spirit in prayer that morning.

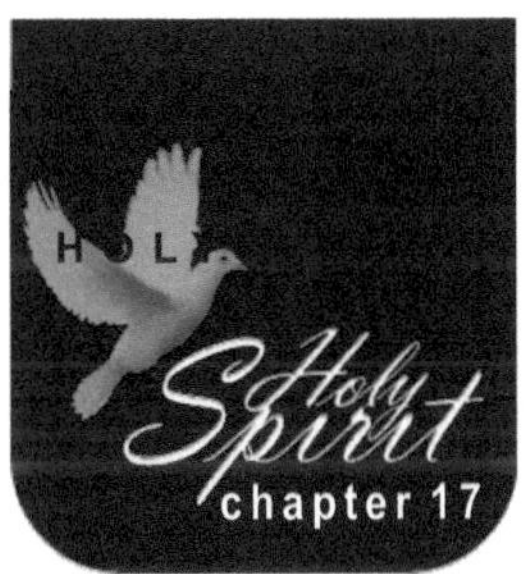

LOW PRESENCE OF THE HOLY SPIRIT IN THE CHURCH

" Thou wilt shew me the path of life: in thy presence is fullness of joy; at thy right hand there are pleasures for evermore". -Psalm 16:11.

"And when they had prayed, the place was shaken where they were assembled together; and they were all filled with the Holy Ghost, and they spake the word of God with boldness." - Acts 4:31.

A young minister was feeling so empty, shallow, dry and used-up in ministry. He was tired and disinterested in spiritual things. He no longer sees revelation whenever he reads the scriptures, nor does he have the passion to pray like before. His heart is cold and things are generally becoming drudgery. While he was questioning in his heart whether he has backslide into sin or not, the Holy Spirit gave him a revelation.

He was taken to a laboratory. There he saw tubes that were filled with water and the water was fresh, clear, clean, and soothing to those it was being used to flow out to wash. At a point, the water in the tube began to go down until the tubes were almost empty. The Holy Spirit now told the young minister that this is his spiritual condition, he was initially filled, but now empty due to constant and regular usage and he has not taken time to get re-filled, the more reason he is experiencing spiritual burnout.

> *When we pray, live holy and commune with the Holy Spirit constantly, His presence will be high in our lives and churches, but when we allow other things, His presence will be low.*

This is a revelation that agrees with the scripture.

"He giveth power to the faint; and to them that have no might he increaseth strength. Even the youths shall faint and be weary, and the young men shall utterly fall: But they that wait upon the LORD shall renew their strength; they shall mount up with wings as eagles; they shall run, and not be weary; and they shall walk, and not faint". - Isaiah 40:29-31.

As it is with individual Christian and minister, so also it is with churches. The presence and power of the Holy Spirit is not always at the same level in our lives and churches. When we pray, live holy and commune with the Holy Spirit constantly, His presence will be high in our lives and churches, but when we allow other things, His presence will be low.

One of the devastating diseases of churches that often results in stagnation, non-growth and apostasy is the abnormal low presence of the Holy Spirit inside the church. It is called 'Hyponeumia' – abnormal low presence and near non-existence of the Holy Spirit in the church which will lead to nominalism, secularization and strong activities of demons inside the church.

Ordinarily, the presence of the Holy Spirit should be high, overflowing and permeating in every local church, which will result in growth, vitality, transformation and turn around

> **"And it came to pass on a certain day, as he was teaching, that there were Pharisees and doctors of the law sitting by, which were come out of every town of Galilee, and Judaea, and Jerusalem: and the power of the Lord was present to heal them".** - Luke 5:17;

> **"Thou wilt shew me the path of life: in thy presence is fullness of joy; at thy right hand there are pleasures for evermore."** - Psalm 16:11.

Because the presence of the Holy Spirit was high among the disciples and in their midst, the place where they prayed was shaken and mighty miracles occurred.

> **"And when they had prayed, the place was shaken where they were assembled together; and they were all filled with the Holy Ghost, and they spake the word**

of God with boldness." -Acts 4:31.

But what do we have today? Why is the presence of the Holy Spirit minimal and very low in our churches today?

a.   **Secular But Educated Preachers**
The church is much more secular today than any other time in history simply because unsaved but highly educated people have been made pastors. Human knowledge, philosophy and educational standard have replaced Spirit-filled and saved people as pastors and leaders of churches.

Many Pastors today are not Spirit-filled and as such run the church with their secular academic qualifications. Pastors who are not baptized and filled with the Holy Spirit will lead the church down. Secular leadership will always produce secular church where the Holy Spirit will fizzle out.

b.   **Doctrine of Cessation**
The presence of the Holy Spirit is very low and minimal in churches that teach and practice the doctrine of cessation; which says that the gift of the Holy Spirit have ceased and miracles have ended with the Apostles after the completion of the New Testament Bible. Such churches have disowned prophecies, gift of tongues, praying for healing and miracles.

Once His presence and Person is denied, He will never be there to bring life and light to the heart and situations of the people.

c.   **Corporate Sins and Disobedience**
When a local church lives in open sins and disobedience to the Lord; whereby sins are tolerated, whitewashed, glossed

over and excused in the church, the Holy Spirit cannot but depart. When the church and her leaders live lives of flagrant disobedience to the word of God and clear instructions of the Lord, then the Holy Spirit's presence will be imperceptible in the church and that will spell spiritual death on every side.

d.   **Grieving, Quenching and Vexing Him**

> **"But they rebelled, and vexed his Holy Spirit: therefore he was turned to be their enemy, and he fought against them".** – Isaiah 63:10

By acts of commission and omission, lots of pastors and leaders in churches have grieved, quenched and vexed the Holy Spirit of God today, just like the Israelites of old and He has become their enemy. One can grief the Holy Spirit through lying, deceit, condoning sins, serving idols of money, fame and twisting the word of God.

You quench the Holy Spirit by disobeying His directions and practicing injustice in the church and you vex the Holy Spirit when you live in immorality and wickedness. And He will fight you and become your enemy! Too many local churches are fighting some perceived enemies in their prayers, not knowing that it is the Spirit of God fighting against them!

e.   **Carnalities and Corruptions**

> **"For the flesh lusteth against the Spirit, and the Spirit against the flesh: and these are contrary the one to the other: so that ye cannot do the things that ye would".** - Galatians 5:17

In churches where there is so much hatred, bitterness, unforgiving spirit, politics and carnal ways of doing things, the presence of the Holy Spirit will never be there in great measure. Human wisdom, carnal, fleshly and worldly way of doing things will always drive away the presence of the Holy Spirit. The flesh will always reduce the presence of the Spirit. And where the flesh reigns supreme, the Spirit will never be in great supply.

f.   Maladministration

Wrong administrative policies that encourage injustice, cheating and shortchanging of workers and staff will always incur the wrath of the Spirit of God. The presence of the Holy Spirit will not be high in a church where favouritism and ethnic bias are subtly encouraged and practiced.

g.   Lack of Fervent Prayers

In churches where the fire of prayers have burnt low or have died out-rightly, then the presence of the Holy Spirit will be abysmally low. When you remove intensive, persistent and heart-felt prayers from the churches, you have successfully limited the presence and power of God in those churches.

h.   Replacing The Word of God

The presence of the Holy Spirit is low in many Charismatic, Pentecostal and denominational churches today because the words of men and ideas of men have replaced the undiluted word of God; then, politically correct messages that tow the middle line, not wanting to offend anyone have taken over many pulpits. Twisting the scriptures to mean something else, thereby teaching error that justifies ungodliness will surely shut the door against the Holy Spirit.

Preaching that motivates, empowers rather than rebuke sin, evil and wickedness of men have not made the Holy Spirit to work in most churches, because the Holy Spirit and the word of God cannot be separated from each other. The word of God is the sword of the Spirit and when the word of God is taken away from a church, the Holy Spirit has been taken away as well!

i.   Members Not Spirit-filled

When majority of the church workers, officers and members are not Spirit-filled, but carnal, unsaved and worldly in their heart and life, the presence of the Holy Spirit will be almost non-existent in that church. It will only be a gathering of nominal, lifeless, powerless and demonized people.

j.   Demonic Agents in Positions

In the quest for growth and financial breakthroughs, churches have cast scriptural standards to the dogs and placed unsaved, ungodly and occultic people in positions of leadership in most churches. And these people have driven out the Spirit of God through their lives, policies and deisms. They are like Simon the sorcerer of old, who wanted to buy the gift of God with money. (Acts 8:13-23).

k.   Lack of Strong Emphasis

Sadly today that Pastors don't lay strong emphasis on new Christians getting baptized in the Holy Spirit. This was quite unlike in the 80's when emphasis on getting baptized in the

Holy Spirit was very strong. If you are not filled with the Holy Spirit then, you are considered a second-class Christian. And that helped us to live holy and seek the Lord earnestly. This lack of emphasis has resulted in weak, anemic and shallow Christians that rise and fall in the faith.

I.   **Misuse of The Holy Spirit**

The presence of the Holy Spirit is also low in the church today due to the fact that preachers now use the gift of the Holy Spirit in their lives to hoodwink, abuse, oppress and destroy the life of others. Some tell lies in the name of the Holy Spirit to marry the wrong person; sleep with widows and take money from people. Some leaders use the term, "the Holy Spirit told me" to keep people quiet and have their way. Unfortunately, leaders who do these have been left by the Spirit of God and the glory has departed from them.

As long as any of the above-mentioned is happening in our churches and personal lives, the mighty presence of the Spirit will be withdrawn and only His token presence will be around. Then, many evils will happen; and flesh and carnality will take over.

The symptoms of the low presence of the Holy Spirit of God in churches are cold, formal and lifeless worship; dryness of spiritual life; powerless and ineffective prayers; oppressive air of bondage; prevailing activities of demons that result in calamities, deaths, nasty occurrences and nominalism.

Furthermore, there will be few manifestations of God's power, barrenness and fruitlessness of the work; lack of guidance and direction and confusion will be everywhere. Stagnation, retrogression and forces of evil will have a field day.

I am sure many local churches can identify with these symptoms today. Even in places that are filled with people, yet these symptoms are in open display. This is a sure sign that the Spirit of God has become a stranger in His church! Even if you gather crowds in your church, and these symptoms are there, it simply means the Lord has withdrawn His presence, just like He did to Samson.

I was involved in a church several years back. The Lord promised to send great revival through the church. Prayers were fervent and we were anticipating great things. But one day, while we the members were praying fervently downstairs, we learnt that our leaders were fighting upstairs. Well, the revival never comes and today, that church is almost empty, bare and lifeless. The Holy Spirit was driven away by the flesh, carnalities, politics, and infighting of our leaders.

Genuine and deep repentance is what we need. Then, we must recognize and fellowship with the Holy Spirit. Turning away from what grieves, quenches and vexes the Holy Spirit is mandatory if He is to return to His church in full force and power. No wonder the Psalmist prayed passionately;

> **"...and take not your Holy Spirit from me"** – Psalm 51:11.

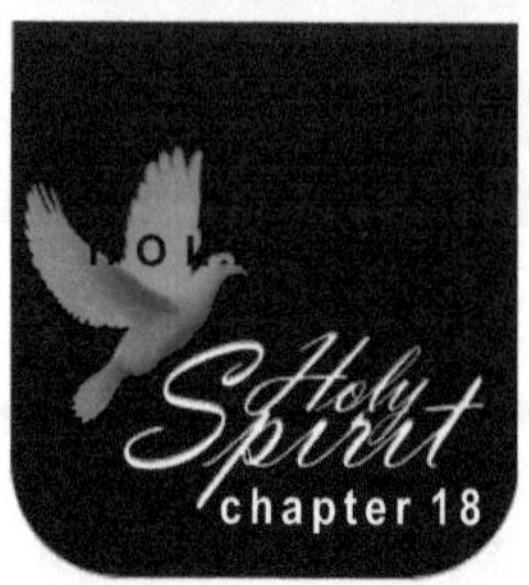

LOW PRESENCE OF THE HOLY SPIRIT,
HIGH PRESENCE OF DEMONS

was once invited to a church to preach. On getting there and being introduced to the altar, my heart and head suddenly went dry and I forgot everything I wanted to say. I tried different strategies to buy time so as to recollect my message, but all to no avail. I had to result to warfare prayers. I made bold declarations to forces of darkness operating inside the church. With that, my message came back and I was able to preach powerfully.

I learnt that day that polluted altars do allow demons to create oppressive climates in the church. Demonic, stifling and oppressive air of bondage inside churches is the direct outcome of the low presence of the Holy Spirit. Once the presence of the Holy Spirit is low, the presence of demons will be very high inside churches.

It is always the desire and plan of the Devil to set up his high places inside each local church, just as he wanted to do in heaven.

"How art thou fallen from heaven, O Lucifer, son of the morning! how art thou cut down to the ground, which didst weaken the nations! For thou hast said in thine heart, 'I will ascend into heaven, I will exalt my throne above the stars of God: I will sit also upon the mount of the congregation, in the sides of the north: I will ascend above the heights of the clouds; I will be like the most High. Yet thou shalt be brought down to hell, to the sides of the pit." - Isaiah 14:12-15.

If the Devil is allowed, either knowingly or unknowingly, he will grab it with both hands. The eternal principle of Satan is 'smite the shepherd and the sheep will scatter' and he follows that by usually targeting the Pastors and the people in leadership. Once the Pastor can be corrupted, Satan will have a great foothold and presence in the church.

The moment any Overseer, Pastor or Leader of a church is smitten by Satan and he or she falls into secret immorality, sexual affairs, lust for money and unscriptural practices, the Holy Spirit will reduce His presence because He is grieved and pronto, the demons will move into the church enmass and very many evil things will begin to take place in the lives of the members and people.

I know Pastors of small, middle sized and large churches that started well with God, but somewhere along the line fell into secret sins of immoralities and lust for money. After some time, demonic presence became pronounced in their churches until things took turn for the worse. These churches are largely mere shadow of their former glory today. They are just too numerous to mention and report is still coming in every week.

Scripturally speaking, the church in Thyatira (Rev. 2:18-25) is a classic example of this. This church started so powerfully in a revival, but relapsed into formalism after sometime and the leadership was corrupted with immoralities until the whole church was corrupted.

When the Holy Spirit is grieved and sent out of our lives and churches though our sins and flagrant disobedience, the devil and his demons will always have free time to operate. Crisis, breakaway, rebellions, disloyalty and bickering will be rife in such churches. Pre-mature death of members, calamities, oppressions, poverty and failures will be pronounced in the lives of the people.

When the presence of demons is high in a church, the people will be spiritually undiscerning, carnal, blind and soundly dead to the things of eternal value. Witchcraft manipulations will be very rife to ruin the finances, marriages, destinies and physical health of the people. At another instance, the church will scatter and become empty. Lots of people will backslide into sin and ungodly living because their faith in the church had been injured.

My private and earnest prayer is not to get demonized. To get demonized is to live in secret sins until the Holy Spirit leaves your life and is replaced by evil spirit, unknowingly. That was the condition that King Saul fell into. He once had the Spirit of God and even prophesied among the prophets (I Sam. 10:10-12), but he got demonized.

The Spirit of God left him and an evil spirit came upon him (I Sam. 19:10). And it went bad for the nation because the leader was demonized; so also with churches and ministries. Many once thriving, lively and dynamic churches have become empty, barren and devoid of spiritual life of God today simply because the leadership have lost the Spirit of God and evil spirits have gained ascendancy. It's time to repent, restitute and be restored!

GLOWING CHURCH OF THE HOLY SPIRIT

" **Thou wilt shew me the path of life: in thy presence is fullness of joy; at thy right hand there are pleasures for evermore."** - Psalm 16:11.

A certain Pastor was really struggling in ministry. He was having a tough time in preparing messages that would bless the people and often times when he preached, he felt that his sermons were dry, powerless and lifeless. The church was also full of infighting, jealousy, bickering and malice. People pitched themselves in camps, for and against the Pastor. Then the Pastor went to a Ministers' Conference where the baptism of the Holy Spirit was emphasized and he believed and got filled with the Holy Spirit.

Immediately, he noticed a difference in his prayer and ministerial life. He was no longer struggling to pray, prepare and preach his sermons. He then made a decision that all his workers must be filled with the Spirit. He gave them one month each to get baptized in the Holy Spirit else, they will cease to be workers in the church.

That was the turning point decision in that church. By the time majority of the church volunteer workers and staff got filled with the Holy Spirit, the atmosphere of the church changed for the better. Spiritual and loving atmosphere was now visible and open heaven of blessings and breakthroughs became a permanent feature of the meetings. Spiritual vitality, discipleship and holy living are always present in the Holy Spirit filled churches.

For the church to truly grow and glow, the Holy Spirit must be mightily present. A growing and glowing church is where godliness, holy living, vitality, permeating air of freedom, revelation, illumination, victory over sin; sickness and Satan are daily occurrence. It is where lives and souls are being saved from the shackles of sin, transformed and edified in the Lord. It is where the Spirit of the Lord is the President and He is allowed to lead, rule and reign without any blockage.

For our church to be a growing church in the power of the Holy Spirit, you must do the following consistently:

a.   **Repentance and Restitution of Climate**
       The negative climate created by sin, hatred and bickering coupled with polluted altars must be repented of and restituted. Allegiance to worldly, occultic and man-made philosophies must be renounced and the Holy Spirit must be recognized and welcomed as the true and only Vicar of the

church.

b. **Renounce, Rebuke and Discipline Sin(s) and Evil**

The Holy Spirit will never stay in a church that condones and tolerates known sins. If you want His greater presence in your church, then you must rebuke and stand against sins. You must be clear and those who live in sin must be disciplined and removed from positions. It was when the first church rebuked and disciplined the sin of Ananias and Sapphira that the Holy Spirit could move freely in the church again.

c. **Spirit-filled Pastors and Leaders**

The greater presence of the Holy Spirit will be seen and known in our churches when the Pastors and leaders are baptized in the Holy Spirit before they are allowed to minister to the people.

It is the overflowing presence of the Holy Spirit in their lives that will spill over to the church. The Apostles were filled again and again and it spilled over to their converts and disciples. You can't give what you don't have.

d. **The Church As House of Prayer**

The presence of the Holy Spirit will be high to destroy all the works of the devil when our churches become the true house of prayer. Prayers that are sincere, fervent and from pure hearts and with godly motives cannot but attract the presence and power of the Holy Spirit.

e. **Holy Spirit Services**

Preach and emphasize the baptism of the Holy Spirit again and again. Constantly seek His infilling and hold services where people can wait on the Holy Spirit to be filled again and manifest His gifts.

f. **Encourage His Gifts**

Welcome His presence in every service. Seek His directions and allow His gifts to function. Don't quench the Spirit in any way. Rather we must pray in the Spirit and use our prayer language often in the church.

g. **Obedient Living**

Teach your people to live obediently according to the word of God. God will only give His Spirit to those who obey and live for Him (Acts 5:32). Disobedient and ungodly living will dry up the Holy Spirit in our lives and the church.

When the presence of the Holy Spirit is high in the church, there will be life, vitality, transformation, amazing miracles and open heaven of blessings. Stagnation will be unheard of and things will move from glory to glory spiritually.

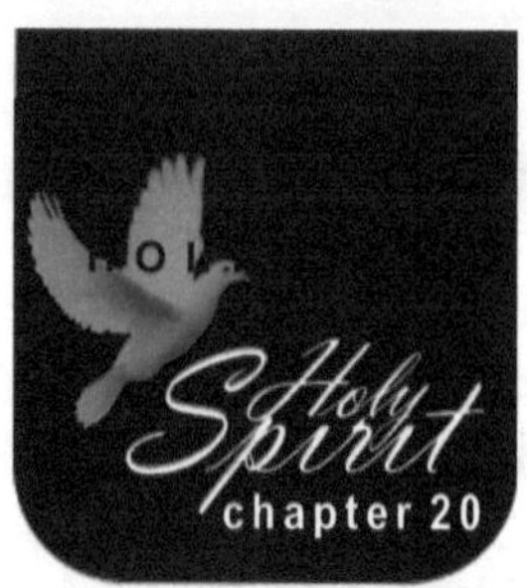

VICAR OF GROWTH

I got converted in a believer's fellowship after a powerful preaching by the man of God. While the preaching was going on, I was being made to see all the sins I have ever committed and when the preacher asked us to confess our sins and invite Jesus into our hearts, I did not hesitate. I prayed sincerely as much as I could and moments later my burden was lifted and joy flooded my heart and soul, and I loved everybody I saw.

From that moment in January 1982, my life changed for the better. I joined a denominational church my elder brother was attending then. Oh what a church! The men and women were on fire, zealous and dynamic for the Lord. The Pastor was an experienced and Spirit-filled man of God. In that church, I knew what it means for the church to be filled and saturated with the presence and power of the Holy Spirit.

There were spiritual atmosphere that made people to fear God, love spiritual things and the word of God was quick and powerful. The services were power-packed and you would never return home the way you came. Weekly, lives were being transformed and souls were being saved. The prayer meetings were something else. The Holy Spirit was directing the prayers and showed us what to pray for. The prophetic messages concerning the present and future purpose of the Lord for the church were accurate. The fire of love for one another was burning brightly in the hearts of the brethren. The zeal for outreach, evangelism and church planting was contagious.

The men of the church were real pillars and spiritual giants for the Lord. The youths were up and doing in the things of the Lord. The Holy Spirit would always reveal the secrets of the enemies and sins in our midst, and once fervent prayers were made, the Lord will always give us the victory.

> *The Holy Spirit is truly the Spirit of growth. He is the One that can bring growth, vitality and spiritual atmosphere that will transform and multiply to the church.*

I remember in a Men's prayer meeting, the Holy Spirit revealed that there was an Achan amidst us and that He would not answer our prayers until we deal with the sin. We stopped praying after the prophecy and asked those involved to confess. Slowly, but surely; a brother rose up to confess his immoral living with married women in his house. He repented in ashes, was prayed for and restored. We later continued with our prayers and the Spirit's presence was mighty in our midst.

Looking back at that church, over 100 of us who were there then have become gospel ministers today, doing exploits in the kingdom. The fundamental truth out of this is that the Holy Spirit is truly the Spirit of growth. He is the One that can bring growth, vitality and spiritual atmosphere that will transform and multiply to the church. It is only His mighty presence that can make the church what the Lord intends her to be. It is when the church is full of the presence and power of the Holy Spirit that the secrets of sins, evil, Satan and ungodliness will never be hidden. It is then quality and quantity growth will be seen.

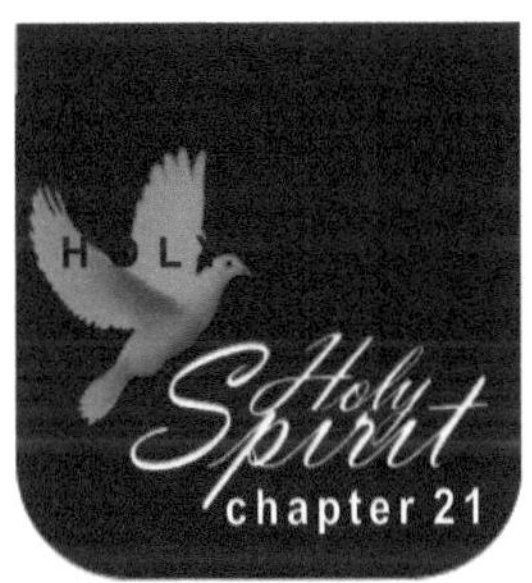

VESSELS OF THE VICAR

"But in a great house there are not only vessels of gold and of silver, but also of wood and of earth; and some to honour, and some to dishonor. If a man therefore purge himself from these, he shall be a vessel unto honour, sanctified, and meet for the master's use, and prepared unto every good work." -II Timothy 2:20-21.

The Holy Spirit is the true Vicar of the church for Jesus. He is the one that appoints men and women and make them physical Overseers of His church; while He is the unseen Vicar that directs things.

"Take heed therefore unto yourselves, and to all the flock, over the which the Holy Ghost hath made you overseers, to feed the church of God, which he hath

purchased with his own blood". - Acts 20:28.

The Holy Spirit is always looking for vessels to use in His onerous assignment of bringing as many as possible to salvation in Christ, maturing them as true disciples, expanding the kingdom of God and getting the church ready for the rapture of the saints.

The Holy Spirit will not anoint chairs, tables, walls, benches and inanimate objects but people. He wants human vessels He can embody and minister through. He wants vessels He can flow into, flow through in a clean, clear, uncontaminated and unhindered way, today and always. He wants vessels He can flow through to preach, heal, deliver, liberate, edify, write, sing and encourage others. As a spirit, He is constantly searching for physical bodies to inhabit and flow through and He wants as many as possible.

> *The Holy Spirit is always looking for vessels to use in His onerous assignment of bringing as many as possible to salvation in Christ.*

Since I learnt this truth many years back, I have secretly prayed to the Holy Spirit to use me as His vessel to bless my generation. I have prayed that the Holy Spirit will preach His preaching through me, pray His prayers through me, write His books through me, minister His ministrations through me and help me to be His sanctified vessel at all times and in all places. And I can say that He has largely answered those prayers, though there is still much more for me to learn and surrender as a vessel of the Holy Spirit.

Candidly, I want to be His vessel to bring revival, restoration and renewal to His ministers and churches across the nation of Nigeria, continent of Africa and the whole world.

Just as the Devil is looking for human vessel to use in his destructive work of making the world a terrible place to live in, so also the Spirit of God is constantly searching for pure vessels to use in bringing glory to God, now and in eternity. Do you desire to be a clean and pure vessel of the Holy Spirit unto honour? Then you must fulfill these qualities:

1.   **A True Vessel Must Be Clean:**
Let the blood of Jesus cleanse you from every sin, evil, ungodliness and unrighteousness. Any dreg of sin in your heart will debar the Holy Spirit from you.

2.   **Surrender Totally:**
You must surrender your totality to Him. He must have control of your life, heart, mind, thoughts and emotions. Don't hold any area of your life back from Him. He must have the whole of you, not half of you.

3.   **Sanctified:**
Your life must be open, transparent and holy unto Him. The Holy Spirit is the pure, holy and righteous Spirit of God. He hates sin and evil. He cannot dwell where bitterness, unforgiving spirit and carnality is dwelling. Therefore, be holy and pure. Let Him sanctify your body, soul and spirit, then you can be His golden vessel.

4.   **Hunger for Him:**
If you feel you can go alone without Him, then you cannot have His gift and presence in your life. You must thirst and hunger for Him, until He fills you

again and again.

5. **Yielded and Pliable:**
   For you to be His golden vessel, you must be totally yielded to His directions and be pliable in His hand. Your will must be submitted to His. You must obey His promptings and guidance.

You will be His mighty vessel when you are constantly drunk and walking in the Spirit. Then He will use you as His mouth, hand, eyes, legs and heart to bring healing, salvation and divine blessings to whoever you come across!

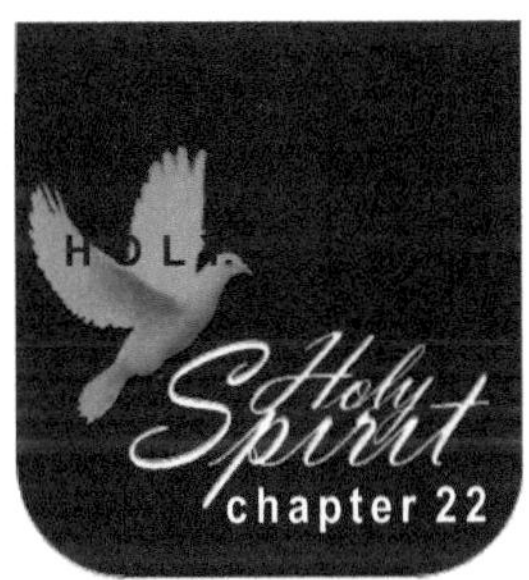

THE HOLY SPIRIT AS SYMBOL OF DOVE

For deep, profound and proper understanding of the person and work of the Holy Spirit of God, we need to study and understand His symbols. The scripture reveals some symbols or emblems of the Holy Spirit. Each of the symbols reveals an aspect of the working of the Holy Spirit. Each symbol represents the working character of the Spirit of God. Not that the Holy Spirit is Dove, Water/Rain, Fire, Wind and Seal, but they represent what He does and can do. They show His working in different aspect in the world.

The Symbol of Dove – Matt. 3:16; Mark 1:10; Luke 3:22.

This is the most popular of the symbols of the Holy Spirit. Lots of churches and ministries use the dove as the logo of their ministries. By symbolizing the Holy Spirit as a dove, there are profound lessons the Lord would want to teach us:-

\# **The Dove At Creation** – Gen. 1:1-3.
In the beginning, we saw how the Holy Spirit was moving over the surface of the earth as a dove would move over its eggs, incubating them. The Holy Spirit was showing Himself as the One who incubated all that God called into being. His brooding produces heat, gestation and creative power. So also He should be allowed to brood over us today thereby incubating the character of Christ in us.

You can't have the Holy Spirit as a Dove upon your life and still be powerless, Christless, lousy and be rough. His dove-like presence over your life will produce powerful traits and character that will make you a mighty blessing to your world.

\# **The Dove During The Flood** – Gen. 8:6-12.
When Noah sent out the Dove the first time, it has no place to land and returned to the Ark. This means that when our lives are full of other things, such as sin, idol worship, worldliness and disobedience to God, the Spirit of God will have no place and would never abide with us, but will go back to God.

\# The second time the Dove was sent out, it came back with a leave or flower; meaning that when you repent and get saved, He would come into you in a small measure. The third time Noah sent out the Dove, it never came back but flew away, because the water has dried up. This means that when we fully receive Him in baptism, He will live within us in fullness and abide forever.

\# **The Dove During The Ministry of Christ** – Luke 3:22; Mark 3:16; John 1:32
The Holy Spirit wanting to do a definite work came upon our Lord Jesus like a dove to anoint Him as a Prophet, Savior and Head of the church. He knew that the Holy Spirit is the Chief Executor of God's work and therefore waited to receive His anointing before commencing the work. Since you believed, has the Holy Spirit come upon you as a dove?

\# **The Dove is a Pure Bird**
The Dove is always white and clean. It hates filth and dirt. So also is the Holy Spirit. He will not come upon a sinner that loves his sin and refuses to repent. The Holy Spirit of God hates sin with perfect hatred and will not abide with a sinner.

\# **The Dove is a Bird of Peace**
The Dove is not violent or harmful. A believer that is filled with the true Spirit of God will be meek, gentle, kind and peace loving (Matt. 10:16; Heb. 7:26; Rom. 16:19). Those who hold grudges, bitterness, vengeful and taking revenge have never known the Holy Spirit as a dove. Those who pray dangerous and terrible prayers to hurt, kill and destroy others are strangers to the Holy Spirit of God. Rather, they are being used by their human and demonic spirits.

> *Not that the Holy Spirit is Dove, Water/Rain, Fire, Wind and Seal, but they represent what He does and can do.*

\#   **The Dove is a Bird Within The Reach of Everyone** – Luke 3:22.
According to the law, it is after you cannot sacrifice a ram or goat due to your poor situation that you will sacrifice a dove. This was the situation the parents of baby Jesus found themselves. And because the sacrifice of a dove is an acceptable sacrifice to God, they brought the dove to the temple. It shows that the Holy Spirit is for all, either poor or rich, young or old, high or low. When you are full of the Holy Spirit, your sacrifice, work and worship will be acceptable unto the Lord.

\#   **The Dove Loves To Be Among its Colleagues** – Heb. 10:25; Acts 1:14.
The dove doesn't fly, eat or sleep alone. You always find them among their companies, chatting, singing and playing together. It's not a bird of isolation. So also when you are full of the Holy Spirit, you find it easier to fellowship, love and relate with the brethren. If you find it hard to fellowship with others, then you need the Holy Spirit afresh.

\#   **The Dove is a Sensitive Bird**
The Dove has spiritual sensitivity to events and happenings. It gives signals of impending danger, calamities and good fortune, so also is the Holy Spirit. There is no secret hidden from Him and if we can truly commune with Him and listen, He will tell us what is in store. He will reveal the plans of the enemy and lead us to avert dangers and calamities.

Are you seeing the tangible symbols of the Holy Spirit in your life as a dove; or the dove has no place to stay in your life?

THE HOLY SPIRIT AS SYMBOL OF ANOINTING OIL

The symbol of the anointing oil is the most misused and misunderstood emblem of the Holy Spirit among Pentecostal preachers today. Some have equated the oil in the bottle with the Holy Spirit, while others have turned to merchants of anointing oil in their churches which everyone must purchase before God will touch them in their area of needs. The anointing oil had been used to anoint anything from cars, houses, and heads of people to both private and public parts of the body and lots of abuses have gone unreported in the name of anointing oil.

A popular minister would always refer to the oil in the bottle as the 'power of God' in your life which you need to guard jealously and continually top-up! That is the height of misuse of this symbol of the Holy Spirit today.

Now, let's look at the scripture concerning this emblem. The oil is not the Holy Spirit, but just an emblem of His work in the life of the saints of God. The oil that will be used for the anointing of priests in the Old Testament must be:

- Beaten out of olives (Exod. 29:40).
- Holy (Exod. 30:25).
- Fresh (Psalm 92:10).
- Pure (Exod. 27:20).
- Precious (Prov. 21:20) and
- Quality (Num. 18:12).

It comes from the mixture of aromatic spices and used to consecrate people and things for the service of God. It is used for the anointing of Priests and kings in the Old Testament and for those who are being prayed for in the New Testament (James 5:16).

Just as the anointing oil is to set people apart to be used of God, so also the anointing of the Holy Spirit is to set us apart for God's work (Heb. 1:9; Psalm 45:7; Isaiah 61:1; Luke 4:18; Acts 10:38).

As the Body of Christ, our Lord was anointed at His burial, signifying that His body in the world must be anointed as with the oil of the Spirit of God (John 19:39-40). There can be a human anointing with oil, devoid of the true anointing of the Spirit of God. Just as king Saul was anointed with a human instrument – a vial or bowl (1 Sam. 10:1), while others were anointed with what was always considered a divine instrument - a horn (Isa. 16:13), indicating a divine anointing. You can pour all the oil in the whole world upon a person, but if the Spirit does not anoint such person, it's a futile effort.

The physical oil percolates, smoothens, melts, saturates, strengthens, energizes and preserves. So also when we have the true anointing of the Holy Spirit, our lives will be able to do all these for others. The anointing oil was not to be poured on just any person. No work of the flesh is blessed by God's anointing. The Holy anointing oil was not to be duplicated in any way (Exod. 30:32); so also we should not succumb to any lie to use any counterfeit anointing for God's work. God's true anointing cannot be gotten by mere pouring of any oil from a bottle, but it's a unique gift from the Spirit of God.

The anointing that comes from the Holy Spirit alone is to cause God's leaders to be able to defeat their enemies (Judges 3:10; 6:34); to be used by God for His purpose, not using the Lord for our own selfish ends; to give us the ability to perform our ministries to the Lord; to bring good news to the afflicted; to bind up the broken hearted; to proclaim liberty to the captives; to comfort all those who mourn; to proclaim freedom to prisoners and to glorify the Lord, not man (Isaiah 61:1-3); and to empower the Christians with the gifts and ministries of the Lord (I Cor. 12; Eph. 4:11-12).

> *Just as the anointing oil is to set people apart to be used of God, so also the anointing of the Holy Spirit is to set us apart for God's work.*

The anointing of the Holy Spirit in a Christian's life comes in different ways and levels. The anointing can be illustrated in any of these ways in the life of the anointed:

*   When God goes beyond the natural abilities of a person and gives supernatural ability to preach, teach and counsel.

*   When a person preaches an entire message spontaneously as quickened by the Spirit (totally different from what he had planned) and the congregation is moved spiritually in a special way.

*   When the conscious sense of God's abiding and moving presence is mightily present.

*   When a preacher's message brings spiritual results in the lives of its hearers even though it might be ungrammatical, unhomiletical, disorganized and unprofessional.

*   When a preacher senses God very near to him and when he is broken or repents of some sins, and then ministers to his people in the same spirit.

*   When the power of the Spirit in the ministry of a leader becomes open and God heals the sick, converts sinners and shows His power through His yielded vessel.

*   When some Christian songs and worship had the touch of God's presence and led people to true repentance.

*   When a minister receives inspiration to write and he can flesh out the outlines of a book in few minutes and cannot shake off the burden until he has finished the writing.

*   When a leader is lifted up in his sprit and ministers the word of God by prophetic illumination and speaks directly to the needs of the people.

* Inwardly sensing through the spirit the specific spiritual or physical needs of a congregation in a church service and ministering to them with God-glorifying results.

* Being sensitive and obedient to the inward leadings of the Holy Spirit, that is never contradictory to His word.

* When the spirit of prayer and intercession comes upon a congregation, and all pray spontaneously as God puts particular burden on individual and corporate hearts.

Whenever a Christian minister experiences any of the above, it is an indicative of the anointing of the Holy Spirit. It is not when ministers do stupid and foolish things like pushing people down, touching their forehead and pushing backward until they lose their balance. It is not when you do 'arranged miracle'; asking people to testify what did not actually happen to them, just to show-off to others that you are anointed!

The true anointing that comes from God will always do things that will edify the people and glorify God. Is the anointing of the Holy Spirit in your life fresh, full and pure? Are you only anointed with physical oil and not the oil of the Spirit of God? Are you only using the anointing oil without the approval of the Spirit of God? It's time to repent and get close to God the Holy Spirit for His true and full anointing that will break every yoke of sin and evil in the world.

**"And it shall come to pass in that day,
that his burden shall be taken away from**

off thy shoulder, and his yoke from off your thy neck, and the yoke shall be destroyed because of the anointing". - Isaiah 10:27.

The true anointing of the Holy Spirit will break yokes, not adding yokes to the life of people.

THE HOLY SPIRIT AS SYMBOL OF FIRE

This is yet another emblem of the Holy Spirit that has largely been abused and misused by charlatans and erroneous preachers who make merchandize of the people today. "Holy Ghost fire" is the most used prayer slang in Nigeria today, both by believers, semi-believers and outright sinners. People invoke 'fire' upon each other and ask their enemies to die by fire!

There are those who labeled themselves as fire, fire apostle and fire, fire church. Their prayer system is 'by fire, by force' even if it's not the will of God. 'Holy Ghost fire' is sent on errands to assassinate their neighbours and those whom they begrudge!

These are distortions of the scripture and wrong use of the fire symbol of the Holy Spirit of God. For the avoidance of doubt, the fire symbol of the Holy Spirit is not to kill, destroy and maim our enemies. The Holy Spirit of God is not for our selfish use at our whims and caprices.

Our Lord Jesus is the One that baptizes with the Holy Ghost and with fire (Matt. 3:11). Baptism with fire means receiving power when you are baptized in the Holy Spirit (Acts 1:8). The fire is to burn in the believer's life, but not to consume him (Luke 24:32; Psalm 39:3 and Exodus 3:1-3).

In the Old Testament, the fire of the Lord was to burn continually in the Temple and never goes out (Lev. 6:12-13). This typifies how the power of the Holy Spirit must forever present in the church. But the time of Prophet Samuel shows the declension in Israel when the fire was going out in the temple (I Sam. 3:3).

Fire denotes the presence and power of God in the Old Testament (Deut. 4:36; Ps. 50:3; 97:3; Isaiah 66:15-16).

*   Fire burns, so also the Holy Spirit fire will burn sicknesses, diseases and every combustible thing in the life of the people. Every minister must be a flame of fire (Psalm 104:4) to burn away sins and problems in the lives of the people.

*   Fire purifies – Mal. 3:3. The fire of the Holy Spirit will purify our lives from any dross of sin and chaff that hinders the Lord.

*   Fire refines – Isaiah 48:10. The Holy Spirit fire will refine our character and transform us into the image of Christ.

*   Fire gives light and reveals the secret of sin – Micah 3:8. When the true fire of the Holy Spirit burns in our churches, the secret of sin and demons will not be

hidden.

*   Instrument of divine justice – Gen. 19:24; Lev. 10:1-2; Num. 11:1; Heb. 12:29. The fire of the Lord was a source of judgment for sinful and ungodly people, so also the fire of the Holy Spirit judges sin, evil and will destroy any strange or counterfeit fire that is not of God. Our God is a consuming fire and will always judge sin with His fiery fire. Therefore, the fire of the Holy Spirit is not what should be trivialized or joked with today.

*   Miracles in the fire – Exod. 3:1-3; Dan. 3:19-25; Acts 4:33. When the fire of the Holy Spirit comes down, miracles, signs and wonders will surely take place in our midst and lives.

The Lord Jesus left the church here for a purpose; winning the sinners back to Him and turning them from the power of Satan to the power of God – Acts 26:18-19. The Lord does not want a powerless church (Acts 1:8; Eph. 6:10), because He knew that we are going to be involved in power encounter.

We cannot make appreciable progress in the ministry or record outstanding result in life without the baptism with fire.

The devil surely has some power (Acts 26:18; Col. 1:8) but the greater power than that of Satan is the power of the Holy Spirit (Matt. 12:28). That is why it is imperative to have the power of the Holy Spirit.

There is a difference between the Holy Spirit and power or

fire. The Spirit is synonymous with power but many have allowed the fire to go out and have only a semblance remaining (Acts 10:38; I Cor. 2:4; Luke 4:1, 14). But it is the will of God that we have the power and fire of the Spirit that will burn sickness, diseases, sins, problems and works of the devil up in people's lives.

We cannot make appreciable progress in the ministry or record outstanding result in life without the baptism with fire (Zech. 4:6). Without the fire of the Holy Spirit burning brightly in our hearts our ministrations and services will not benefit the people. It will largely look like a child's play, customary and powerless.

The only way the fire or power of the Holy Spirit will manifest in our lives and ministries is when we spend time fasting, praying and waiting upon the Lord. Jesus is the baptizer in the Holy Spirit and fire. As you take time to wait upon Him in fasting, fire from the altar will fall upon you afresh. The power of the Lord will come upon you afresh as you take time to seek His face (Matt. 17:21). You can only feel the fire of the Holy Spirit by consistent prayer and fasting.

This has been my experience in the last 30 years of my Christian life and in the ministry. There are times I worked so hard and busy until I will begin to feel empty, tired and burnout. I will then take time to seek Him afresh and after some days, His fire will return and the work will move forward again. The power of the Holy Spirit or His fire is not for us to use for our selfish ends. Rather, it is what we must be sober with and seek His leading as to how He wants to manifest through us. Surely, our God is a consuming fire! (Heb. 12:29).

Is the fire of the Holy Spirit still burning in your heart and life? Is the fire of the Lord burning brightly or very low in your church? Are you using Holy Ghost fire to kill, murder and destroy your perceived enemies? Or are you using the fire of the Holy Ghost to burn sicknesses, sins, diseases and ungodliness away in the heart and life of people?

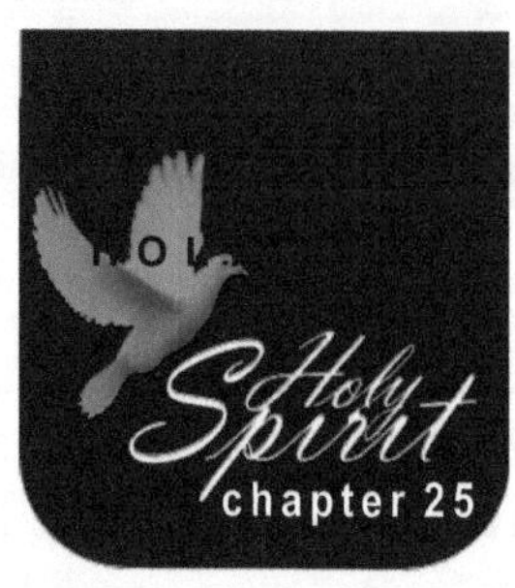

THE HOLY SPIRIT AS SYMBOL OF THE WIND

"The wind bloweth where it listeth, and thou hearest the sound thereof, but canst not tell whence it cometh, and whither it goeth: so is every one that is born of the Spirit." – John 3:8

"And when the day of Pentecost was fully come, they were all with one accord in one place. And suddenly there came a sound from heaven as of a rushing mighty wind, and it filled all the house where they were sitting. And there appeared unto them cloven tongues like as of fire, and it sat upon each of them. And they were all filled with the Holy Ghost, and began to speak with other tongues, as the Spirit gave them utterance." - Acts 2:1-4.

One other scriptural symbol of the Holy Spirit is that of WIND. In the last three symbols we have studied, we have seen the tremendous truths that were revealed through those emblems. We shall look at this symbol again with a view to reveal more aspect of the workings and manifestations of God the Holy Spirit.

The wind is a powerful agent of nature.

> **"And as they departed, Jesus began to say unto the multitudes concerning John, What went ye out into the wilderness to see? A reed shaken with the wind?** – Matt. 11:7;

> **"And he said, Go forth, and stand upon the mount before the LORD. And, behold, the LORD passed by, and a great and strong wind rent the mountains, and brake in pieces the rocks before the LORD; but the wind: and after the wind an earthquake; but the LORD was not in the earthquake".** - 1 Kings 19:11.

Even though we could not see the wind nor take hold of it, yet the facts of its existence are proved by the work it does; much more is the Holy Spirit of God, though we could not see Him, yet, He exists and works.

There is absolutely nothing that can withstand the power of the wind. (Matt. 7:25-27; Psalm 1:4).

> **"Behold also the ships, which though they be so great, and are driven of firce winds, yet are they turned about with a very small helm, withersoever the**

governor listeth". - James 3:4.

"The north wind driveth away rain; so doth an angry countenance a backbiting tongue". - Prov. 25:23.

It blows everything out of its way. A case in point is the Tsunami that ravaged South East Asia few years ago. It carried water high up and blew away houses, trees and leveled everything in its part. The wind has absolute power that nothing could withstand its ways or hinder it wherever it is blowing. So also is the Holy Spirit of God. When He is at work, nothing can withstand nor stop Him.

As there are North wind (Songs of Solomon 4:16); South wind (Acts 27:13); West wind (Exod. 10:19) and East wind (Job 27:21), so also the Holy Spirit is all over the four corners of the earth.

In Europe and America, the power of the wind has been harnessed through windmills to bring electricity to communities and nations. The wind carries so much power and it is this power that is used to generate electricity. The wind power of the Holy Spirit brings light to darkened hearts, places and communities when we allow Him to operate.

Degrees of Manifestation

a.   **Gentle Breeze**

"And God remembered Noah, and every living thing, and all the cattle that was with him in the ark: and God made a wind to pass over the earth, and the

waters assuaged" - Gen. 8:1.

This is the lowest degree of manifestation. It gently sways and brings freshness and coolness to the body. This is the common and frequent manifestation of the wind. It is a daily manifestation. So also we have the gentle wooing and swaying of the Holy Spirit in the hearts of both sinners and saints everyday.

> *The wind has absolute power that nothing could withstand its ways or hinder it wherever it is blowing. So also is the Holy Spirit of God.*

b.   Strong Wind

"But let him ask in faith, nothing wavering. For he that wavereth is like a wave of the sea driven with the wind and tossed." -James 1:6.

This is the moderate compelling force that bows down and rocks trees and houses. It compels things to bow down and do its bidding (Psalm 147:18). So also there is this strong wooing of the Spirit that compels sinners to repent and believers to take the step of obedience.

c.   Mighty Wind

"And suddenly there came a sound from heaven as of a rushing mighty wind, and it filled all the house where they

were sitting". – Acts 2:2

"Thou shalt fan them, and the wind shall carry them away, and the whirlwind shall scatter them: and thou shalt rejoice in the Lord, and shalt glory in the Holy One of Israel." - Isaiah 41:16

This is the most powerful manifestation of the wind. It is called whirlwind or Tsunami. It uproots trees, houses and destroys whatever stands in its path. What we greatly need today is this mighty gale wind of the Holy Spirit to bring down revival and sweep away all the corruption, coldness, lukewarmness and worldliness of the church.

When we have the mighty wind of the Holy Spirit manifesting, souls shall be swept into the kingdom in large numbers; souls shall be directed to the church from the four corners of the earth (Num. 11:31). Life will be brought back from the dead (Ezek. 37:9); those running away shall be arrested (Jonah 1:4) and the enemies of the Lord shall be dealt with (Exodus 15:10).

When we have the mighty wind of the Holy Spirit, we shall experience spiritual transportation as was Philip (Acts 8:39-40). When we have the mighty wind of the Holy Spirit, there shall be revival and wonderful acts will be performed. The church will be swept clean of false doctrines, false preachers and ungodly churches will be turned back to become His church.

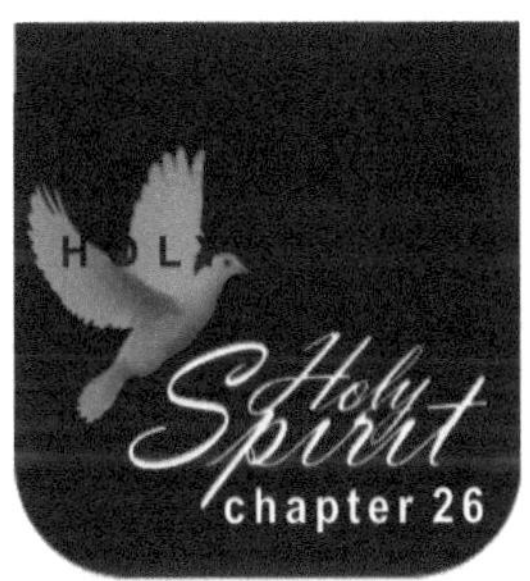

HOLY SPIRIT AS SYMBOL OF WATER OR RAIN

❝In the last day, that great day of the feast, Jesus stood and cried, saying, If any man thirst, let him come unto me, and drink. He that believeth on me, as the scripture hath said, out of his belly shall flow rivers of living water. (But this spake he of the Spirit, which they that believe on him should receive: for the Holy Ghost was not yet given; because that Jesus was not yet glorified.)" – John 7:37-39

Another wonderful symbol that demonstrates the work of the Holy Spirit is water. Jesus says that he who is thirsty should come and drink and out of such shall flow out rivers of living water.

The Book of Ezekiel chapter 47 verses 1 to 6 equally shows water flowing out from the altar. At first, it was ankle level, then knee, loin's level, until it became over flowing river that one can swim in. Such is also the presence of the Holy Spirit in our lives. We can move from ankle level to over flowing level of His presence and power.

*   Water gives life – The Holy Spirit is also life-giving.
*   Water refreshes – The Holy Spirit refreshes your spirit daily.
*   Water cleanses – The Holy Spirit springs cleansing and purity to our hearts.
*   Water is indispensable – No believer can live for God without the Holy Spirit.
*   Water gives fruitfulness – No one can be fruitful in Christian life and service without Him.
*   Water puts an end to drought – With rain and water in abundance, there will be no room for drought in our lives and work.

All these are wonderful descriptions of the work of the Holy Spirit. When we are full of Him, we shall experience all these and be able to bring it to others. The person who is full of the Spirit shall have living waters flowing out of him to meet the needs of the world. And the promise is to whosoever will be obedient to the Lord.

HOLY SPIRIT AS SYMBOL OF SEAL

"And grieve not the holy Spirit of God, whereby ye are sealed unto the day of redemption" – Ephesians 4:30

The Holy Spirit is the One that is keeping the believers secured for the Bridegroom. He is the One that has sealed us, kept us and marked us different and completed for the coming Bridegroom

"Who hath also sealed us, and given the earnest of the Spirit in our hearts."
-II Cor. 1:22.

* A Seal is a mark of ownership
* A Seal is for security.
* A Seal is for safety purposes.
* A Seal is for preservation.

All these He is doing for us so that the wicked one will not be able to touch us. He is the One hindering the Anti-Christ from appearing until the saints are taken away at rapture. He is the one preventing Him from touching us and keeping him at bay (2 Thess. 2:6-9).

He is the seal that keeps every believer safe and secure in Christ and will escort the church to meet the Lord in the air on the day of rapture. He is the one that has saved us from the wrath to come and kept the saints by the power of God today.

> **"Who are kept by the power of God through faith unto salvation ready to be revealed in the last time."** -1 Peter 1:5.

As long as you are indwelt by the Holy Spirit, you are one of His and are being kept by Him. You must however, remain in Him also and keep yourself away from what will make Him leave your heart and life.

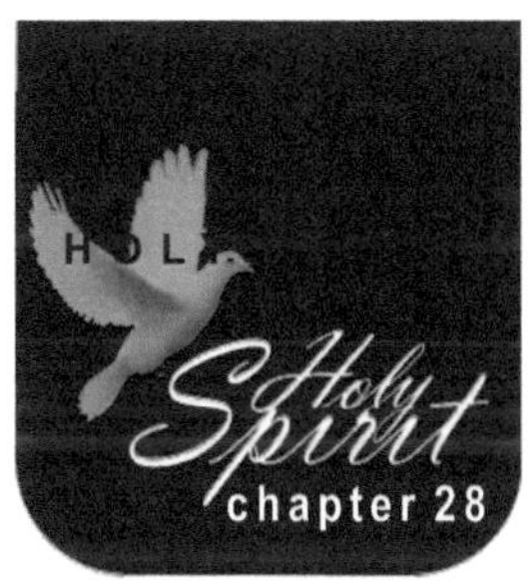

THE FRUIT OF THE SPIRIT

The Holy Spirit used Apostle Paul to balance the teaching of the gifts of the Spirit by adding a love chapter (1 Corinthians 13) in between the teaching. This shows that we are not to be one sided. We are to hold both the gifts and fruits in proper balance. The gifts can only be beneficial and realize their full potential if they are manifested in Love to God, Others and Myself.

MEANING OF THE FRUIT OF THE SPIRIT

These are the gracious and Godly habits produced in the life of a consecrated believer who has been baptized and filled with the Holy Spirit (Gal. 5:22-23). Note that "the works of the flesh" in Galatians 5:19 are plural, but "the fruit of the Spirit" is singular because evil passions are many and varied, while the fruit of the Spirit is unified in purpose and direction. The nine graces called the fruit of the Spirit could be grouped into three:

a.   In relation to self,
b.   In relation to neighbour and
c.   In relation to God.

A.   **IN RELATION TO SELF**

The first three graces are love, joy and peace. These are the states which I experience in my own heart. They directly affect me. The first part looks inward.

1.   **Love:**
        The Greek equivalence is 'Agape'. This is divine love, an attribute of the indwelling God. (1 John 4:26). Divine love 'Agape' is the tender, compassionate devotion to the well-being of others. It is the sacrificing of oneself and things for the benefit of others. (John 3:16; Rom. 4:8; 1 John 3:16; 4:19; 1 Cor. 13:4). Love is the mother of all other fruit and graces. The rest grew out of love, 'Agape'.

2.   **Joy:**
        This is not the joy of alcohol or material possession, but deep gladness in the spirit. It is not mere natural cheerfulness, but the unfailing lightness, brightness and calmness of the heart given by the Holy Spirit. (Psalm 43:4; Isaiah 61:10). It is also called the "rejoicing hope" (Heb. 3:6); the "joy of faith" (Phil. 1:25). This spiritual joy is permanent (John 16:12; Phil. 4:4) and unspeakable (1 Peter 1:8). The joy of the Lord is our strength (Neh. 8:10).

3.   **Peace:**
        This is the tranquility which is shed abroad in the heart by the sense of one's reconciliation with God.

(Rom.5:1; II Cor.5:18-20). It is the peace of God that satisfies the soul completely. (Col. 3:15). Love, joy and peace reveal a perfect order. Love is the foundation, Joy is love singing and Peace is love resting. (Rom. 14:17).

B.   IN RELATION TO MY NEIGHBOUR

The second group of graces comprise of longsuffering, gentleness and goodness. These are Christian dispositions that should be displayed towards others. They constitute how the Christian relates with his neighbour.

4.   **Longsuffering:**
This is patient endurance even in the face of provocations. Patience and endurance are the natural characteristics of the saints. Unbelievers are very impatient (1 Cor.13:4-7; Col. 1:11; Eccl.7:8; Rom. 12:12; II Tim 4:2).

5.   **Gentleness:**
A Christian in the spirit should be gentle, softspoken, kind-hearted, refined in character and conduct (II Tim 2:24-26; Titus 3:1-2; James 3:17). Jesus Christ is known by His gentleness, and Christians should follow His example (Heb. 7:26).

6.   **Goodness:**
The Christian should be good, kind, virtuous, benevolent, generous and Christ-like in lifestyle and conduct. Goodness makes the Christian full of good works (Titus 2:14; Prov. 24:21; Matt. 5:44; Luke 6:27; Rom. 14:20; I Thess. 5:15).

Longsuffering, gentleness and goodness are in order. With love, there will be longsuffering. Gentleness is longsuffering in passive expression. Goodness is longsuffering in active expression.

C.   **IN RELATION TO GOD, MY MAKER**

The third group is faith, meekness and temperance. These are attitudes which the Christian should maintain as the very first essentials of godliness. They have special reference towards God.

7.   **Faith:**
This speaks of Christian faithfulness. He is dependable and can be relied upon at all times. God is faithful to all His promises; therefore the Christian should be faithful in all his callings (1 Kings 8:56; I Cor. 4:2; Heb 3:2).

8.   **Meekness:**
It means kindness and patience in suffering injuries without feeling a spirit of revenge. It is characteristic of Jesus (Matt.11:29; II Cor. 10:1). Believers are commanded to be meek and to show a lowly spirit one to another (Col. 3:12; Eph.4:2).

Meekness is the true mark of a humble heart. He is lowly, self-effacing, submissive, teachable, not proud, arrogant, boisterous, bragging, heady and high-minded.

9.   **Temperance:**
It means self control. The Christian should show moderation in the indulgence of the appetites and

passions. We must be moderate in dressing, habit and fashion. (Prov. 23:1-3; 25:16; Rom. 13:14; Titus 2:2). We must be moderate in our eating habit (Phil. 3:19).

Self control is the law of life, while self indulgence is the law of death (1 Cor. 9:27).

The Christian character is not just a legal correctness like the Pharisees. It is the possession and manifestation of the fruit of the Spirit. Taken together, they present a "moral portrait of Christ". The Holy Spirit is the One that builds and fashions out this character in the life of the Christian. The more we welcome and fellowship with the Holy Spirit, the more He will transform and make us into the image of Christ, with all the fruit of the Spirit glowing brightly in our lives (II Cor. 3:18).

You don't force the fruit of the Spirit to manifest in your life. It should be a natural result if you are full of the Holy Spirit. If the fruits are not in your life and showing forth in your character and attitudes every day, then you are not filled with the Holy Spirit of God, but with other spirits.

THE GIFTS OF THE HOLY SPIRIT

The gifts of the Spirit, though manifested in the Old Testament were not in much quantity as after the Spirit was poured out on Pentecost. The ascension of Christ was specifically to release our benefits and poured them out on us. These privileges have been since the foundation of the world, but tied and caged by sin until Christ liberated them for us (Rev. 5:1-10; Eph. 1:4; 4:8).

Every believer has been given a gift by God and you are in trouble if you don't use it (Matt. 25:24-30). However don't confuse spiritual gifts with the following:

1.   **Natural talents** – God may sometimes transform a natural talent at salvation into a spiritual gift.

2.   **Fruit of the Spirit** – It is the indispensable foundation on which all gifts are exercised.

3.   **Christian roles** – There are roles you play but not empowered by the Holy Spirit.

4.   **Counterfeit gifts** – There are lots of fake gifts on display, not showcasing godly living.

Importance of These Gifts to The Church

1.   It demonstrates the supernatural power of God (Prov. 18:16). It is through these gifts that the power of God will manifest in the church.

2.   It reveals the presence of God in the church. The Lord usually shows up through the gifts.

3.   They made the church to be afraid of sin, knowing their secrets will be revealed. Where the gift of the Spirit is in operation, secrets of sin and the enemies will be exposed.

4.   The church would not be in darkness as to the plan of the enemy. We shall not be blind to the works of darkness with the gifts of the Holy Spirit manifesting.

5.   The church will be edified and Christ glorified. His gifts will definitely bring glory to His holy name.

6.   Miracle will be a daily occurrence with the presence of the gifts of the Holy Spirit.

7.   The work of God will be easy and interesting. There will be liveliness in the work of the ministry with the gifts of the Spirit.

The church of Christ will thrive more with the gifts of the Holy Spirit in operation. Every Pastor must operate in at least three gifts for the church to be growing and healthy. Members and leaders must also operate in the gifts of the Holy Spirit, though it must be done in order and respect to unity in the church. However, we must not quench the Spirit by placing embargo on gift usage in our fellowships.

Spiritual Gifts

A spiritual gift is a special attribute given by the Holy Spirit to every member of the Body of Christ according to God's grace for use within the context of the Body.

Spiritual gifts are extraordinary grace-gifts of the Holy Spirit bestowed on sincere Christians for special services. Through these supernatural abilities, the believer is able to accomplish the will of God for his life or in the life of others.

> *The church of Christ will thrive more with the gifts of the Holy Spirit in operation.*

The Greek word for gift is 'Charismata' - meaning gifts of grace (not worked for). Everyone has at least a gift. Not self-choosing but sovereignty distributed by the Holy Spirit of God. All are honourable and work by same Spirit (I Cor. 12:4-7, 11).

The purposes of these charismatic gifts are threefold:
a.   To build up the body of Christ - Eph. 4: 11-13.
b.   To edify the Saints - I Cor. 12:4-7.
c.   To convict and convert the sinners - 1 Cor. 14: 12-25; Acts 2: 12.

Though I would be majoring on the nine gifts mentioned in 1 Corinthians chapter 12, yet I would not limit myself to only this passage of the scripture. There are controversies over the actual number of gifts or ministries in the Bible.

So for the sake of broadness, I shall be looking into passages like Romans chapter 12 and Ephesians chapter 4 verses 11 to 13. All these ministries and gifts are given by the Holy Spirit and they will be to our benefit if we consider them in brief. I shall treat this under two broad headings; MINISTRY and GIFTS.

A.   **MINISTRY:**

These are ministry-gifts to be leaders in the body of Christ. None is above the other, they are to help each and complement one another.

1.   **Apostle:** Eph. 4:11; I Cor. 12:28; Acts 2:43; 13:3; 14:14; Rom. 16:7
An Apostle is one sent forth with orders; a delegate or an ambassador; a bearer of a commission or a charge. He is a pioneer.
   i.   An Apostle must have seen Christ (II Cor.12:12; I Cor.14:18).
   ii.   He must possess sign gifts.
   iii.   He must be called by God (Rom. 1:1).

   Functions:
   i.   To establish local churches; He is an explorer (Rom. 15:20).
   ii.   To be a spiritual father to others.
   iii.   To bring forth revelation of the word.

iv.   To train and discipline ministers.

2.   **Prophet:** Eph 4:11; 2:20; Acts 13:1-4; Acts 11:27-30; I Cor. 14:29-33 A
A Prophet is a foreteller of God's word and future events; also a forth-teller of God's word under inspiration of the Spirit; a mouthpiece or spokesman for God and an interpreter of God's word.

Functions:
i.   To function in the office of a Prophet.
ii.   To pronounce judgment on evil.
iii.   To edify, exhort and comfort the saints.

The simple gift of prophecy should not be confused with the prophetic office. In the simple gift of prophecy, one cannot function in the office of a Prophet. To be a Prophet, the gifts of revelation must be added to prophecy. To prophesy only does not make one a Prophet. There must be gifts of wisdom, discernment of spirits, and word of knowledge with signs to be a Prophet. Prophets should not be driven out today since they were in the church in the beginning (Acts 13:1-2; 11:27-28; 21:10-13, 33).

3.   **Evangelist:** Eph. 4:11; Acts 21:8, 2Tim. 4:5.
He is a preacher of the gospel. A preacher having a harvesting ministry. One who can present the gospel in a simple, clear and understandable way. He is an itinerant preacher (Acts 8:40).

Function:
i.   To win the lost through preaching and miracles.

ii.   To go to where the sinners are.

iii.   To train soulwinners.

iv.   To start and establish local churches with Apostolic teams.

The gift of Evangelist is one of the major gifts given to the church today. The gospel is to be preached to the whole world by every Christian; but God gave the gift of Evangelist to some in order to bring multitudes to Himself.

4.   **Pastor/Shepherd** - Eph 4:11; John 10:16; John 21:16, 1 Peter 5:2-3; Psalm 23.
     A herdsman of God's people; an overseer of the church; one who tends, guards, feeds and guides the flock of God.

     Functions:
     i.   To feed the flock (with proper, appropriate and balanced diet).
     ii.   To counsel the flock.
     iii.   To lead the flock (both by practice and precept).
     iv.   To identify with the flock (in every need and circumstance).
     v.   To oversee a local flock (by Prayer-intercession, counsel and teaching).
     vi.   To train and help the flock to reproduce.

5.   **Teacher:** - 1 Cor. 12:28; 2 Timothy 2:2, 23; Acts 13:1; Eph. 4:11.
     A Teacher is an instructor of God's word; one who is able to impart knowledge in a systematic way; a teacher of other teachers.

Functions:

i. To establish truth and doctrine from God's word.
ii. To teach other teachers how to teach.
iii. To correct doctrine and detect errors.
iv. To balance out the inspirational ministry of both the Prophet and Evangelist.

These are the major leadership and ministry offices that were apparent in the New Testament Church. They are all related to one another. The Prophet sees Macedonia, where the church is to be established. The Apostle is informed. He organizes the church workers and the Evangelist to go and preach there. The converts won are given to the Pastor. The Teacher is to assist the Pastor in nurturing the converts.

However there are other minor, yet important ministries-gifts in the church. Among them are:

6. **Giving** - Rom 1:11; 12:8; Eph. 4:28.
    One who shares and imparts what he has with others very liberally. One whose ministry is to give to others out of the abundance that God has given to him or her.

Functions:

i. To meet others' needs through giving.
ii. To believe God for blessings so that others may receive them in turn.
iii. To give financially and sacrificially to meet the needs of the church.

7. **Ruling:** - Rom 12:8; I Thess. 5:12; 1 Tim. 3:5, 12.
    This is one who presides over different church functions; one who is able to take the lead by good examples and ability to help. One who is able to organize, facilitate and administrate over church activities.

    Functions:
    i.   To protect or guard the flock with a Leader's instruction.
    ii. To take the lead in church activities.
    iii. To be a support ministry to the Pastors of a local church.
    iv. To organize and carry out activities and programmes.

8. **Helps** - 1 Cor. 12:28.
    One who is able to give relief and help; one who is able to console, encourage and strengthen others. One who is able to lighten the load of certain leaders by doing certain practical things for them.

    Functions:
    i.   To help in practical ways in a local church.
    ii. To relieve some of the everyday needs of people in the church.
    iii. To relieve those who serve in the word of some of their routine responsibilities.
    iv. To give to meet needs anonymously.

9. **Intercession**: - Isaiah 59:16; Rom. 8:26-27, 34; 11:2; 1 Tim. 2:1.
    This is one who confers with or entreats another person: one who goes to meet a person for

conversation, consultation or supplication.

Functions:

i. To pray for others with a supernatural revelation of their needs.

ii. To bring the needs of the church before the Lord with a special fervency and frequency.

iii. To have a deep prayer life and ministry which God uses as a speaking vessel to bring certain needs before Him.

10. **Singer**: - 1 Chronicles 15:16, 19, 27; 2 Chronicles 5:12-13; 9:11; 20:21; 23:13; Eph. 5:19; Col. 3:16, Heb. 2:12.
One who is a strolling minstrel; one who inspires the people of God through a song; one who is able to make a melody to the Lord with his or her voice.

Functions:

i. To glorify God in a song.

ii. To be an active member in the church choir.

iii. To lead the church's song service.

iv. To inspire others to sing the song of the Lord.

v. To sing the song of the Lord with the anointing of the Spirit.

vi. To be a special soloist in song to edify the church.

11. **Door-Keeper:** - 1 Chronicles 9:17-26; 15:18, 23-24; 16:38, 42; 26:1, Psalm 84:10
One who waits at the threshold/door of the church.

Functions:

i. To have a special ministry of greeting visitors as they arrive at the church building.

ii.   To help people find seats in the congregation
iii.   To be an Usher.
iv.   To serve the congregation in similar ways.

B.   GIFTS:

The list of the 'Charismata' is in 1 Corinthians 12:4-11,28-30. The nine manifestations of the Spirit to be discussed now are divided into three distinct divisions as follows: Just like the fruit of the Spirit, the gifts of the Spirit are grouped into three trios:

a.   **GIFT OF REVELATION (MIND GIFTS)**
1.   The word of Wisdom.
2.   The word of Knowledge.
3.   The Discerning of spirits.

b.   **GIFT OF INSPIRATION (VOCAL GIFT)**
4.   Prophecy.
5.   Divers kinds of Tongues.
6.   Interpretation of Tongues.

c.   **GIFT OF POWER (MIRACLE-WORKING GIFTS)**
7.   Faith.
8.   Gifts of Healing.
9.   Gift of miracle.

These gifts are to support and confirm and help the call of God upon our lives.

a.   **GIFT OF REVELATION (MIND GIFTS)**

1.   **The Word Of Wisdom -** I Cor. 12:8
     This gift operates by the ability to perceive and

communicate how the ways of God apply to a specific situation. It is to function and speak under a supernatural mantle of wisdom and prudence; to receive from the Lord specific understanding as to the best way to handle a situation or problem (Matt. 10:19-20).

The gift of wisdom is different from general wisdom. Wisdom is always consistent with the will of God. Here are some scriptural examples; Matthew 22:17-22; John 8:3-9; 1 Samuel 16:2-3; Acts 6:10; Genesis 44:15-16, 25-32.

These are some of the instances that the word of wisdom was in operation both in the Old Testament and New Testament. We need this gift today to solve knotty and perplexing problems.

The word of wisdom like the word of knowledge can come through:
i.   Inward revelation.
ii.   Audible voice.
iii.   Vision and dream.
iv.   Prophecy.
v.   Angelic visitation or
vi.   Tongues with interpretation; through feeling also.

The word of wisdom is a revelation pointing to the FUTURE about the plan and purpose of God.

2.   **The Word Of Knowledge** - I Cor. 12:8; 5:3-5
This is being able to receive from God supernatural facts and information which would otherwise be

humanly impossible. Ability to communicate the truth by divine revelation of the specific facts about a situation; and to communicate to others the specific mind of God for a situation and to reveal to others or group their specific needs by divine revelation.

This gift of knowledge does not come by natural ability, observation, study, education or experience. It is God's gift. Basically, the word of knowledge brings a revelation concerning things past or present and sometimes future. It is also used to reveal sickness and demonic oppression or possession.

Scriptural examples are: 2 Kings 5:20-27; 2 Kings 6:8-21.; Acts 5:1-11; John 1:47-50; 4:16-19; 20:19,20,20-28; Matthew 16:6-11; Acts 8:26-30; 21:10-13; 2 Kings 6:32-33; 7:1-2.

The gift of knowledge is not natural intelligence. It is the God-given ability to know the truth about a vexing situation that cannot be known by natural means. This gift is indispensable to any preacher and church so that we will not be in darkness to secret sins, problems and activities of devils and coming events.

3. **Discerning Of Spirit** – 1 Cor. 12:10
    This is being able to recognize what spirit (divine, evil or human) is behind a certain manifestation or activity.

    To judge accurately what is of the spirit of God and what is not. To have a gifted, sensitive spirit so as to be able to distinguish between truth and error and to be able to know spiritual source behind something or someone.

Scriptural examples are: Acts 16:1-18; 13:6-12.

We need this gift today so that we will not be fooled. We need to know which spirit is working through people, whether Divine, Satanic or Human.

b.   **GIFTS OF INSPIRATION (VOCAL GIFTS)**

4.   **Prophecy** – 1 Cor. 12:28; 12:10
This is to speak in an understandable language inspirationally to men's exhortation, edification and comfort. To encourage Christians through the anointing of the Spirit. True prophecies are not conceived by human thoughts or reasoning (2 Peter 1:21; 1 Cor. 4:4).

Prophecy is a gift for every Christian and one of the gifts of a Prophet, not all. The three fold reasons of prophecy are:
I.   Edification
ii.   Exhortation and
iii.   Comfort - 1 Cor. 14: 3.

The Holy Spirit speaks to rebuke or exhort in a gentle manner. It should not be used for personal glory, or pointing or dragging people in the Church.

Seven Ways To Judge Prophecy
a.   By fruits - Matt. 7:16-20
b.   Does it glorify Jesus? -John 16:12-14
c.   Is it in line with the Bible? -Isa. 8:20

d.   Does it come to pass? –Deut. 18:20-22
e.   Does it give freedom or put into bondage?
f.   All are not of God -Deut. 13:1-5
g.   By spiritual discernment -1 John 2:20, 27

5.   **Tongues** - 1 Cor. 12:10; 14:5-6, 18, 21-23, 27-28, 39.
      This is speaking by the spirit in language not previously learned. To speak out a supernatural utterance and which will be interpreted by same or different person in a public gathering of the church for edification. To speak a language not previously learned by formal education that is understood by the hearers. (Acts 2:4, 8-11; 10:46; 19:6).

      The gift of tongues is different to the sign of reception or baptism of the Holy Spirit. Tongues at Holy Ghost baptism is a sign. But the gift is for our personal edification and Church. Here you can speak shortly but at the gift you can speak and sing continuously.

      The gift of tongues enables us to communicate directly to God. This is praying beyond our human understanding. It is the 'hotline' to heaven. The tongues should not be used to cause confusion in the Church. When there is no interpretation we should speak to ourselves and to God (1 Cor. 14:19, 28). The tongues in Acts chapter 2 are full of worship, obedience, unity, edification and orderliness. But the one of Babel is full of confusion, rebellion, division and blasphemy against God.

      The gift of tongues is for personal edification (1 Cor. 14:4, 15; Jude 20). We are to build up or charge our battery by speaking in this our beautiful prayer language. It is the sign that the Holy Spirit is dwelling in us.

6. **Interpretation Of Tongues** - 1 Cor. 12:10, 30
This is being able to speak the truth supernaturally the interpretation and meaning of a message in tongues in the church. To interpret the meaning of a message given by the gift of tongues in a congregation. This is both inspirational and spontaneous. The regulation for speaking in tongues includes the services of an interpreter.

Private Use: Sometimes, God through this gift may permit us to know certain things we have been praying for in our private devotions in other tongues (1 Cor. 14:2, 13-15). Such interpretation may be uttered forth in form of prayer or in form of an affirmation or declaration.

Public Use: An utterance in tongues in a public service by the prompting of the Holy Spirit is allowed (1 Cor. 14:5). If there is no interpretation, then control the volume and speak moderately to God and to yourself (1 Cor. 14:26-28). Stop also when others stop (1 Cor. 14:32).

The purpose is to profit the Church. Before the church can be edified the message from the Lord must be clear (1 Cor. 14:6-13).

One who is used in interpretation should be in tune with the Spirit as another person is making utterances in tongues. Enter into the spirit of worship and be open to be filled with God's presence. Understand that tongues with interpretation means prophecy (1 Cor. 14:5). The gift of tongues and interpretation were the only two gifts that were not manifested in the Old Testament.

C. **GIFTS OF POWER (MIRACLE WORKING GIFTS)**

7. **Faith** - I Cor. 12:9
    This is to believe God for the impossible; special faith for what God has promised to do and an ability to see it come to pass.

    It is to receive from God supernatural power to believe Him for miracles and to speak the word of faith with results. It is called "Faith in God" (Mark 11:22) by the Lord. Others call it "Faith of Miracles" - it is an inspired faith from God in the life of the gifted Saint. It is such faith that moves mountains into the sea (Matt. 17:20; Mark 11:23).

    Other scriptural references are; Matthew 21:19; Genesis 22:8; 1 Samuel 14:6; 1 Samuel 17:37; 1 Kings 17:1-7; Mark 4:37-41.

    The gift of faith is different from the general faith of all saints. This gift is extraordinary confidence in God to achieve a set purpose and objective in line with God's will. The gift of faith is not concerned with historical but with the future; that is why some people call it vision and dreams.

8.   **Healings** - I Cor. 12:9, 28-30; Acts 4:22-30.
This is to be the instrument through which God brings healing or a cure. To be able to lay one's hands on others and see them restored to health by the power of the Spirit on regular basis. To be able to be the instrument through which God's power heals a special kind of sickness most all of the time.

A person who does not believe and hold on tenaciously to the doctrine of divine healing cannot have this gift.

In Mark 16:17-18, it was given in a little measure to believers as a sign to heal the sick, but you have the full measure when you have the gift. The gift of healing restores health gradually and speedily while miracles are automatic and instantaneous (John 5:2-9).

Essentials of This gift
i.   **Faith:** The manifestation of this gift cannot come without faith. (Heb. 11:6; Matt. 17:14-21).
ii.   **Much prayer and fasting:** If we don't pray and fast regularly and consistently we cannot see the manifestation of this gift and other gifts. (Matt. 17:21).
iii.   Unbelief will hinder the manifestation of this gift (Mark 6:1-6).

Ways to use the gift
The gift of healings can be manifested and experimented with in various ways according to the leading of the Spirit of God. We cannot stereotype

the Spirit if we want His manifestation. We must therefore be open to Him.

i.   By laying of hands - Matt. 8:14-16; Mark 16:17-18
ii.   By anointing oil - James 5:14
iii.   Prayer of faith – James 5:15
iv.   The name of Jesus - Acts 3:1-11
v.   By cloth - Acts 19:11-12
vi.   Water

If you are canal, glory-seeking and self-centered, God cannot give this gift to you. However we need it today because about 80% of the third world people are afflicted with one ailment or the other.

9.   **Miracles** - 1 Cor. 12:10, 28
This is one who has been given with a ministry of power and deliverance. It means to be able to perform the supernatural through the power of God, to do something not normally possible with nature by the power of God to the glory of God.

Scriptural references are; Mark 2:12; John 2:1-11; Mark 4:39; Luke 7:11-17; Daniel 3:22-25.

The parting of the Red Sea, the Manna, Water from the Rock, the stopping of the Sun and moon are a few of the miracles of God in the Old Testament. Miracles do not always involve healings. They are signs and wonders and mighty deeds which should accompany the witness of the gospel (John 4:48).

The purposes of miracles are:
i.   To display God's power and prove that God is alive (Heb. 13:8).

ii.   To destroy Satan's work (1 John 3:8; Acts 10:38).

iii.   To bring glory to God (John 2:11; Matt. 15:30- 31; Luke 7:11-17).

iv.   It proves the divine authority of the miracle worker was sent by God (Exod. 4:1-5; John 3:2).

v.   It makes men listen to God's message (Acts 8:6; Rom. 15:18-19).

HOW THE GIFTS ARE RECEIVED AND KEPT

a.   RECEIVING:

1.   Submission of one's life to the will of God.
2.   Live and dedicate your whole life. (2 Tim. 2:19- 21).
3.   Receive the Holy Spirit If the gifts are of the Spirit, then we must receive the Spirit (Acts 1:8).
4.   Desire the supernatural. In your desire check your motives, are they selfish, canal or godly? (1 Cor. 12:31; 14:1).
5.   Prayer and fasting (Acts 13:1-4).
6.   Move with gifted people.
7.   Accept God's wisdom. It is his gift and He will give it as He deem fit (1 Cor. 12:7, 11).
8.   Launch out in Faith (1 Kings 8:44).

b.   KEEPING THE BLESSING

It is common for man to lose precious gifts especially those they did not labour for. But we are enjoined to keep ours (Rev.2:25; 3:11).

c.   HOW TO LOOSE YOUR GIFT

1.   Pride
2.   Praise loving
3.   Position Seeking - 3 John 9-10.
4.   Talkativeness
5.   Much eating - Gen. 25:29-30.
6.   Grieving the Spirit by disobedience
7.   Lack of self control
8.   Prayerlessness.

d.   HOW TO KEEP THE GIFT

1.   Watchfulness in small or great things – SoS. 2:15
2.   Don't give room to any sin.
3.   Don't follow worldly standard or people.
4.   Looking unto Christ - Heb 12:2.
5.   Keeping the altar fresh -Phil 3:7-17

Keep your consecration and love for the Lord, seek the Giver than the gifts.

More explanations on the role, place, power, process and manifestations of the gifts of the Spirit will be given in my forth coming book, **"FIVE FOLD MINISTRY"** Check it out!

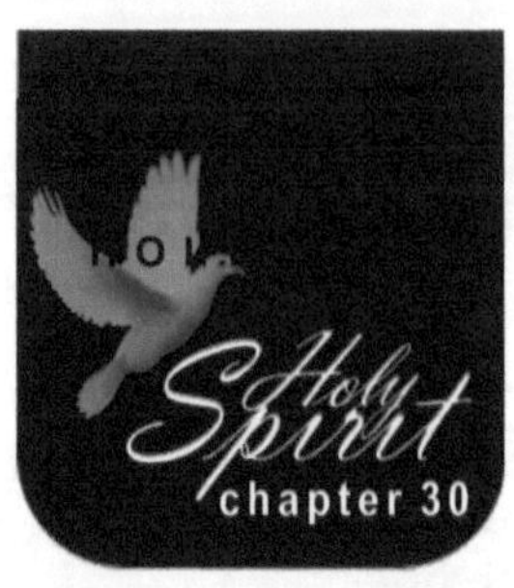

LEADINGS OF THE HOLY SPIRIT

"And, behold, there was a man in Jerusalem, whose name was Simeon; and the same man was just and devout, waiting for the consolation of Israel: and the Holy Ghost was upon him. And it was revealed unto him by the Holy Ghost, that he should not see death, before he had seen the Lord's Christ. And he came by the Spirit into the temple: and when the parents brought in the child Jesus, to do for him after the custom of the law," – Luke 2:25-27

Simeon is a Jewish believer that was very devout and the Holy Spirit was leading him. He was led by the Holy Spirit to know that he would see Jesus alive before his own death and was equally led by the Spirit at the right time into the temple to see the baby Jesus. This shows that the leading of the Holy Spirit is imperative in the life of every Christian. The

Holy Spirit seeks to lead every believer into the will of God. (Romans 8:14).

Every believer must seek the clear, definite and direct leading of the Holy Spirit in every area of their lives. It has been noted that there are only two types of people when it comes to leading: Objective people and Subjective people.

Objective people seem to be led by their reasoning, logical and rational senses, thinking and outward evidences. They take their decisions based on their thinking and logical reasoning; and there are lots of Christians like that. They don't really believe in being led by the Spirit, rather they use their senses, thinking faculties and outward evidences to lead. Unfortunately, they have missed the best of God for their lives.

The subjective people however seek to be led by an inner voice, nudging and irrational thoughts. They rely more on their intuition and inner witness than logical, rational and reasoning faculties. The subjective people seem to have much more positive results in their lives than the objective ones. Relying on your gut, intuition and inner voice of the Holy Spirit will save you 8 out of 10 times in your decision making process.

Every believer must humbly pray, submit our heart and plans to the leading and direction of the Holy Spirit. I have really enjoyed the leading and leadership of the Holy Spirit in my life and ministry. Whenever I seek His guidance, He has never failed to provide it.

A particular case is when I needed to resign from my former church in order to face the Church Growth Ministry fulltime.

Though I felt I should resign, but I still sought His guidance and He led me to wait two more years before I finally tendered my letter of resignation. And within those two years, there were series of events that happened and by the time I resigned, He has provided a good platform for me to fully begin the Church Growth Ministry.

The Holy Spirit can lead you in several ways. He can speak to you through the inner voice, a dream or series of dreams; He can choose to give you an angelic visitation, or send someone to you with prophetic word or speaks to you through the printed pages of the Bible or through a preacher while preaching. Whichever way He chooses to speak to you, what is important is that you recognize His voice and know the way He has chosen to lead you.

> *Every believer must humbly pray, submit our heart and plans to the leading and direction of the Holy Spirit.*

It is sad to note that many Christians and ministers have failed to know and recognize the leading of the Holy Spirit in their lives. They are like young Samuel of old, who did not recognize the voice of God (1 Sam. 3:4-7), until he went to Prophet Eli.

Inability to recognize the voice of the Holy Spirit has made many to make terrible mistakes. Some have mistaken the leading of their own human spirit for that of the Holy Spirit and have gone against the word of God. That is why you hear people saying that they are led to divorce their wives, sleep with church members, marry unbelievers and drink alcohol.

Sometime ago, one of the topmost church leaders in Nigeria traveled to the United States. There, he met the General Overseer of a particular church in Nigeria who had earlier won Visa Lottery and relocated to the U.S., leaving his church back home with his Associates. On getting to the U.S., he had nothing doing and was therefore re-ordained by the top church leader as one of his Pastors. He was then made to pastor one of his branches over there.

When the top church leader came back to Lagos, the Associates of the General Overseer asked him why he re-ordained their leader as one of his Pastors. He simply replied that he was led by the Holy Spirit. But events later proved him wrong.

When you fail to recognize and separate the voice of the Holy Spirit from other voices, you will fall into grave errors and regrets. The Holy Spirit will never lead you against the word of God. He will never lead you to do things you will later regret. Therefore, check every leading you receive with the word of God and with Spirit-filled and matured leaders. He will never lead you to abandon your wife, children or husband for ministry or vocational work.

The leading of the Holy Spirit is gradual and continuous in our lives. If you learn to obey His small promptings, He will continue to give you greater leadings. If you disobey, ignore and quench His leadings, He will stop speaking to you. Your continuous prayers, listening and obedient living will greatly help His leading to be clear and greater in your life.

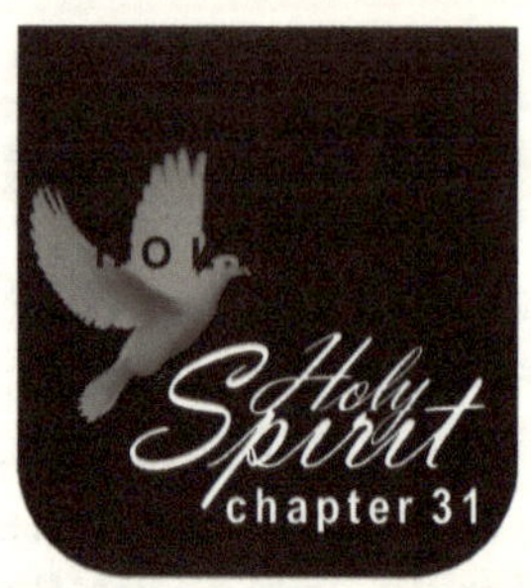

THE FLESH VERSUS THE SPIRIT

"But they rebelled, and vexed his holy Spirit: therefore he was turned to be their enemy, and he fought against them." – Isaiah 63:10

"This I say then, Walk in the Spirit, and ye shall not fulfil the lust of the flesh. For the flesh lusteth against the Spirit, and the Spirit against the flesh: and these are contrary the one to the other: so that ye cannot do the things that ye would. But if ye be led of the Spirit, ye are not under the law." – Galatians 5:16-18

Few years back, I saw a Magazine with the caption; "20 Fastest Growing Churches in Nigeria". Of course, I was interested and bought it. Perusing through the stories of those churches, I discovered that 16 of them have cases in court. While they seem to be growing numerically to outsiders, internally, they are battling with carnalities, works of the flesh and demonic activities. I'm sad to report that majority of those 20 churches are crawling, stagnant and on a downward spiral today, due principally to those works of the flesh that have gained ground among them from within.

The flesh, carnal tendencies and besetting sins will always quench the Spirit of God. God's Spirit and fleshly pursuits cannot work together. It is either we mortify the flesh so that the Spirit can have free way to work, or allow the flesh to quench the work of the Spirit in our lives and in the church. When the Bible says in I Thessalonians 5:19 "Quench not the Spirit", it simply means we should subdue our fleshly tendencies so that the Spirit of God can have a free reign in our lives and churches.

It is however quite sad to note that fleshly desires and carnal tendencies have been allowed to disturb, disrupt and debar the flow of the Spirit of God in the churches today. Envying, jealousies, politicking, tribal sentiments and disloyalties have been elevated to prime positions in the scheme of things and the Spirit of the Lord had been grieved.

Fleshly wisdom and strategic political maneuverings have been used to corner positions, titles, monies; and carnal people have replaced Spirit-filled Christians in sensitive positions, thereby driving out the Spirit of the Lord from the church.

The Holy Spirit will never abide where there is every evil work and devilish wisdom.

"But if ye have bitter envying and strife in your hearts, glory not, and lie not against the truth. This wisdom descendeth not from above, but is earthly, sensual, devilish. For where envying and strife is, there is confusion and every evil work". - James 3:14-16.

Infighting, bickering, animosity and internal wars will always quench the Spirit of God in the church. Disunity, disloyalty, rebellion and backstabbing will never allow the work of God to thrive in our hearts and life.

Recently, I heard the story of two Senior Pastors in a particular denomination who were internally fighting each other over snide comments during transfer to each other's churches by their General Overseer. These two Pastors do greet each other, but are inwardly fighting each other in the last 10 years! You can imagine the spiritual damage they would have done to those under them.

I also remember the case of a Pastor who broke away and took the branch of the church he was sent to. He and his erstwhile Overseer married from the same family and they often attend the same Ministerial Fellowship. Outwardly, they seem to be friends, but inwardly they were fighting and devouring each other. This went on from 1976 till 2007 – a whole 31 years, yet they were pastoring people. By the time we visited them to broker peace and reconcile them, lots of damages have been done to their personal lives, people and churches.

Furthermore, fleshly and carnal behaviours have been used to drive out gifted, dynamic and outspoken young people in the church. Leadership has trampled over people with great potentials and they have left the church and downward spiral have set in.

The Spirit of the Lord will never dwell where the flesh is reigning. If we really want the Spirit to work in us and through us, then we must mortify all fleshly attitudes. We must put on the Lord Jesus, walk in the Spirit and make no provision for the flesh.

> **"Let us walk honestly, as in the day; not in rioting and drunkenness, not in chambering and wantonness, not in strife and envying. But put ye on the Lord Jesus Christ, and make not provision for the flesh, to fulfil the lusts thereof"**. - Romans 13:13-14.

No matter how Spirit-filled you are, once you allow things of the flesh to have the upper hand, you are driving out the Spirit of the Lord in your life and church.

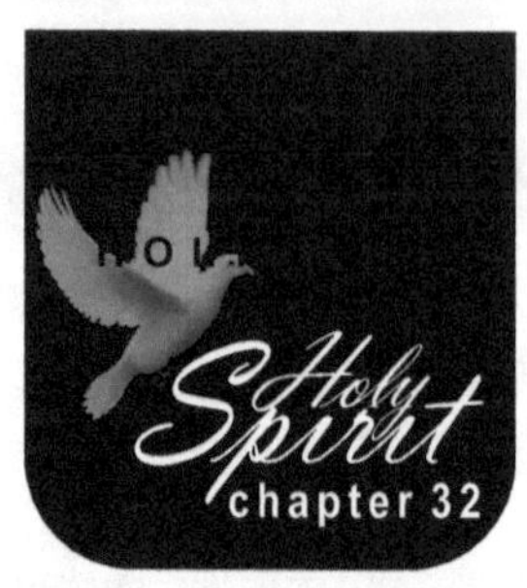

THE HOLY SPIRIT – REVEALER OF SECRETS

> **"But God hath revealed them unto us by his Spirit: for the Spirit searcheth all things, yea, the deep things of God. For what man knoweth the things of a man, save the spirit of man which is in him? even so the things of God knoweth no man, but the Spirit of God."**
> - I Cor. 2:10-11

After I became born-again and filled with the Holy Spirit, I needed to solve a personal problem. The problem is that I don't know my exact date of birth simply because my parents did not keep accurate record when I was born. Upon learning that the Holy Spirit can and do reveal secrets, I decided to seek the Lord in prayer to help me solve the problem of my exact date of birth. I went to my late mother, told her and she was able to confirm it. And that is the date of birth I had been using since. This was a great boost to my faith that there is no secret hidden from the Lord.

The Holy Spirit is a revealer of secrets, either the secret things of the Lord or secrets of the hearts of men. There is nothing that is hidden from Him

"The secret things belong unto the Lord our God: but those things which are revealed belong unto us and to our children for ever, that we may do all the words of this law". -Deut. 29:29.

He does reveal secret things to those who seek Him sincerely and are deep in communion with Him. He can reveal past secrets of what has happened and future secrets of what He wants to do. He is the one that reveals the secret that Ananias and Sapphira kept and exposed their lying (Acts 5:1-4).

Too many people are living secret-driven lives today. Though they come to the church, yet there are secrets in their lives that hinder the Lord from working and blessing them. Until they confess these secrets, they will continue to wallow under God's judgment, anger and curses. While some are aware of their secrets, others are blissfully unaware of the secret pacts, covenants, incidents and dedications that have kept them in bondage for years. And it is the Holy Spirit of God that can reveal these secrets, either through Spirit-guided preaching of the word of God or prophetic insight.

When the Holy Spirit is allowed to work in a church or fellowship of people, He loves to reveal hidden things. It is then people will really know that God is really at work in the church

"And thus are the secrets of his heart made manifest; and so falling down on his face he will worship God, and report that God is in you of a truth." -I Cor. 14:25).

In one of my former pastorates, I remember the Lord dealt with us bountifully along this line. Secrets of hearts were being revealed on a daily basis through the undiluted and Spirit inspired preaching and teachings of the word from the Holy Spirit. What a time of exciting growth we had in that church. At a point, my people knew that whatever evil they did in their homes and offices will be revealed by the Lord whenever they get to church! It made everyone to be afraid of sin and thereby lived right! It is however sad today, that many Pastors don't want the Holy Spirit to work to this extent in their church because they themselves have secrets of sins.

Welcome the Holy Spirit in full measure to your life and church. Give Him the pre-eminent place in the scheme of things. Allow Him to lead and relinquish control to Him. Ask Him to be in the driving seat and take time to fellowship with Him, and then He will reveal secret things. He will not cover the secrets of evil, backsliding and sins in the lives of the people. He will expose all that will not allow Him to work and once we can deal with those things, then He will reveal more until glory will come and cover us all.

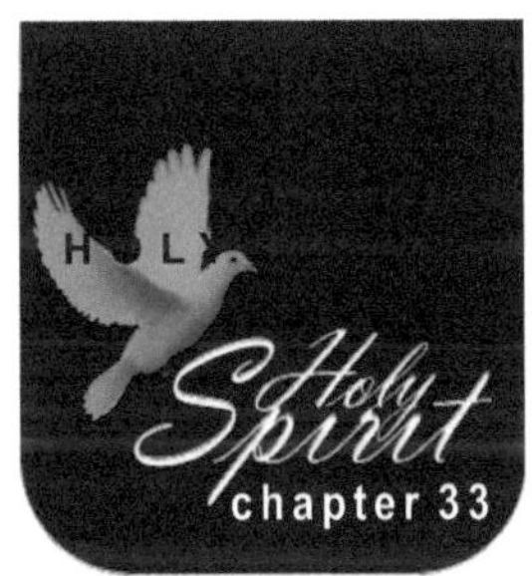

GROWING IN THE SPIRIT

"If we live in the Spirit, let us also walk in the Spirit. This I say then, Walk in the Spirit, and ye shall not fulfil the lust of the flesh." - Galatians 5:25, 16.

"For he that soweth to his flesh shall of the flesh reap corruption; but he that soweth to the Spirit shall of the Spirit reap life everlasting." - Galatians 6:8

We are not a spiritual being on an earthly journey, but a spiritual being on a spiritual journey to our eternal home. Every Spirit-filled Christian is a spiritual being housed in a body. It is mandatory then to tune always to our spiritual being and stop living in the flesh. The Bible commands us to live and walk in the Spirit. And that can only be possible when we are so Spirit-filled, drunk and drenched and then do everything by the leading of the Spirit of God.

Walking in the Spirit is to mortify the works of the flesh and renounce every worldly and carnal entanglement. It is to allow the Holy Spirit to mould our character and form us to the image of Christ. As you wash in the blood of Christ and swim in the water of the word of God everyday, the Spirit will be transforming you to the very image of Christ. He will build your character with the fruits of the Spirit and produce Christ-likeness in you. He will shave off touchiness, irritations, impatience, envy, jealousies and every unbecoming trait. He will make you a good person.

It takes time and humility of heart to grow in the Spirit and things of the Lord. It is difficult for so many because they have learnt over the years to depend only on their senses, thinking, learning and faculties. To now humble themselves and depend solely on the guidance, inspiration and insights given by the Holy Spirit of God is too humbling for them. The more reason many professed Christians would rather depend on what they see than the Spirit they don't see. And that is why they don't grow in the Spirit and spiritual things.

> *To truly grow and live in the Spirit, you must be disciplined and self-denying.*

To truly grow and live in the Spirit, you must be disciplined and self-denying. You must embark on the journey of personal growth. You must improve, update and upgrade yourself, knowledge and relationship with the Lord and people. You must never be contented or satisfied with where you are or who you are. You must dip yourself in the things of the Lord and work on your spiritual life. You must run away from too much eating, talking, sleeping, playing and too much pleasure. All these things leak away the Spirit from your heart and life. Growing in the Spirit demands for absolute dedication to the Lord and things of eternal value.

You must pray in the Spirit by speaking in tongues and seeking the Lord's leading before you take a step or decision. Growing in the Spirit demands that you don't walk like mere men, but see things from scriptural and heavenly perspectives. It is being heavenly minded and eternity conscious in all your actions, thoughts and reactions.

You will grow in the Spirit, walk and live in the Spirit when you move with men of the Spirit. Who you move with will determine your spiritual state. If you move with fleshly men, you will be carnal and reap corruption, but if you move with spiritual men and women, you will grow in the things of the Lord. It takes conscious effort, intentional and purposeful decisions to grow and walk in the Spirit. I bet you, no life is more exciting than the life in the Spirit of God. Being in the Spirit is a supernatural life where nothing is impossible.

> **"I was in the Spirit on the Lord's day, and heard behind me a great voice, as of a trumpet"** -Rev 1:10

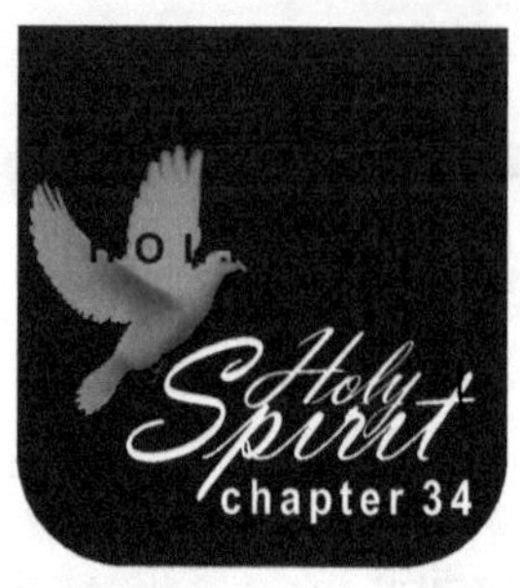

THE HOLY SPIRIT AND PRAYER

"Praying always with all prayer and supplication in the Spirit, and watching thereunto with all perseverance and supplication for all saints;" - Ephesians 6:18

"Likewise the Spirit also helpeth our infirmities: for we know not what we should pray for as we ought: but the Spirit itself maketh intercession for us with groanings which cannot be uttered." - Romans 8:26

The Holy Spirit is the Spirit of prayer and intercession. We are to pray in the Spirit and intercede through the Spirit. He helps us to pray as we should and it is in intensive prayers that He manifests Himself. There is no better soil to cultivate the Spirit of God than that of prayer.

The Holy Spirit moves in prayer, works in answer to prayers and manifests Himself and His gifts mightily through the atmosphere and avenue of prayer. Without intensive prayers therefore, the Holy Spirit cannot and will not work mightily in our lives and churches. It is only when intensive, protracted and prevailing prayers are abounding in our lives and churches that the Holy Spirit will be able to work mightily. This is one lesson I have learnt over the last several years.

As a young Christian, I was introduced early to prayer and I was a strong member of the prayer team of our local church.

We hold vigils thrice a week and determine what happens in the church during our prayer times. Whenever our prayers are intensive, we see the Spirit of God working mightily in the church. At other times when we are cold, lukewarm and listless in our prayers, He will not work so mightily, ditto to my personal life.

I can recollect a time we decided to embark on three months fasting and prayers for the church, with vigils. It was tough but very spiritually rewarding and enriching. The Spirit of the Lord worked so mightily in the church, subsequently; growth was visible on every side. Oh that our churches can be true house of intensive and Spirit-guided prayers, then the days of God's power will be here again!

Your church must pray and prayer must become a ministry in the church.

One of the major ways we quench the Spirit of God is by neglecting prayers. Prayerlessness is a major sin against the Holy Spirit. Yes, there are lots of routine, official fireless, powerless and passionless prayers today, but they don't move the Sprit. Your life and church must pray from holy hearts, burning desires and faith-filled minds for the Holy Spirit to be moved. You must build a personal life of prayer, early morning, late at night and sometimes, all night in prayers. It is by personal, regular and consistent life of prayer that you can be filled with the Spirit and He can flow unhindered through you.

Your church must pray and prayer must become a ministry in the church. There must be House of Prayer, regular times of Corporate Fasting and Prayers; School of Prayers and Ministers of Prayers. These prayers must encompass all facets of prayers; intercession, petition, thanksgiving, binding and loosing and importunate. It is then the Spirit of God can really work to save, heal, deliver and transform people in the church.

The Spirit will always work in commensurate to the prayer life of the Pastor and the church. Prayers give the Holy Spirit the legal and Biblical authority to invade our lives with God's blessings. The atmosphere of prayer allows the Holy Spirit to cleanse, purify and renew our hearts and churches.

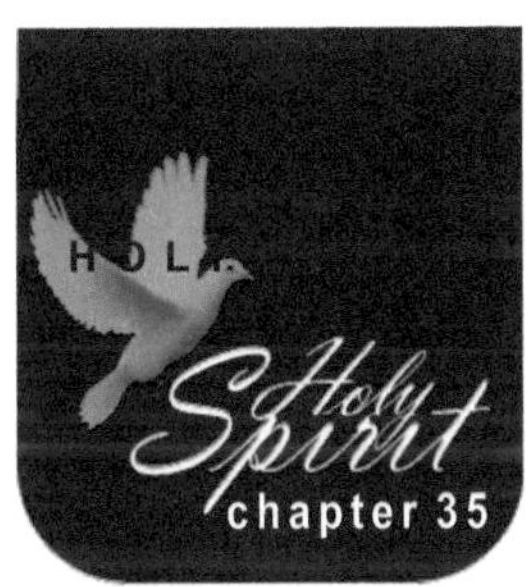

THE HOLY SPIRIT AND WORD OF GOD

"And take the helmet of salvation, and the sword of the Spirit, which is the word of God:" - Ephesians 6:17

"For the word of God is quick, and powerful, and sharper than any twoedged sword, piercing even to the dividing asunder of soul and spirit, and of the joints and marrow, and is a discerner of the thoughts and intents of the heart." - Hebrew 4:12

As a Preacher, Pastor, Teacher and Church Consultant of many years standing, I have seen and continue to see the place and power of the word of God in transforming the lives of people for good. When preached under the strong influence of the Holy Spirit, the word of God is truly quick and powerful to bring transformation to hearts, lives and churches.

The word of God is the broom of the Holy Spirit to sweep clean the lives of people. The work of the Holy Spirit in the world is to touch hearts, cleanse lives free from sins, pollutions and purges away the evils of the world from the hearts of God's children. And the most effective and permanent way He does it is through the undiluted word of God. He will always use the instrument of the word to uproot from the heart all the evil plants of the devil and corruptions of life.

"Whose fan is in his hand, and he will throughly purge his floor, and gather his wheat into the garner; but he will burn up the chaff with unquenchable fire". -Matt. 3:12

"But he answered and said, Every plant, which my heavenly Father hath not planted, shall be rooted up". - Matt. 15:13

The word of God is equally the sword of the Spirit to cut asunder into the hearts, emotions and marrows of the mind. Without the word of God in our lives and churches therefore, there would be nothing for the Holy Spirit to use in cleansing, purging and winning victory for us. Without the truth of the word of God being boldly declared, the Holy Spirit is incapacitated to work in the church.

Unfortunately, majority of the churches of today are Biblically illiterate. The word of God is diluted, innovated, muddled up and watered down so as to make merchandise of the people. The ideas of men, motivational talks and secular orientations have been used to replace the undiluted truth of God's word today, the more reason lives are reformed but not Holy Spirit transformed today.

The Holy Spirit cannot work the work of transformation in the hearts of people with the ideas of men and secularized preaching in majority of the pulpits of today. That is why truly saved, transformed and victorious living is a rarity among the professed Christians of today. Lots of churches have programmed out the word of God from their meetings. Dancing, singing, worship, giving and other things have been used to replace or shorten the time given to the word of God. Preaching time is abysmally short and only a short secular talk on quotable quotes.

I'm even aware of a Denominational church that would not allow speakers to open and read from the Bible, during plenary sessions in their Pastors' Conference! Yet, it is labeled a Pentecostal Church! By so doing, the Holy Spirit was effectively hindered from working in the church. And heavy darkness fell on and pervaded the denomination during the tenure of that leader.

The undiluted word of God, not the letter, but the Spirit is the instrument of the Holy Spirit to wash the church clean. The word as water must be much to purify and cleanse from all sins and evil. The growth of the word of God will lead to the growth of the church (Acts 6:7; 19:20).

"And the word of God increased; and the number of the disciples multiplied in

Jerusalem greatly; and a great company of the priests were obedient to the faith." - Acts 6:7

"So mightily grew the word of God and prevailed". -Acts 19:20

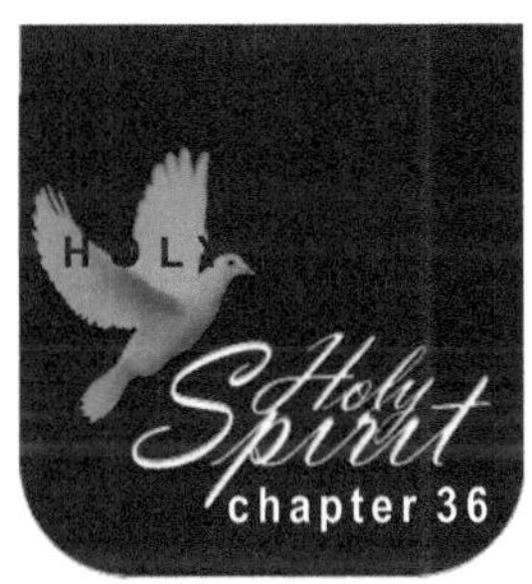# THE HOLY SPIRIT AND THE KINGDOM OF GOD

❝For the kingdom of God is not meat and drink; but righteousness, and peace, and joy in the Holy Ghost.❞ - Romans 14:17

The subject of the kingdom of God is still largely a mystery to so many Christians. Yet, the scripture is not in doubt about the kingdom of God. The kingdom of God is not in the future but now.

"And when he was demanded of the Pharisees, when the kingdom of God should come, he answered them and said, The kingdom of God cometh not with observation: Neither shall they say, Lo here! or, lo there! for, behold, the kingdom of God is within you." - Luke 17:20-21

The kingdom of God is the rule and reign of God in the heart of His people. It is not a geographical boundaries, nor kingship of men, rather, it is the Holy Spirit spreading the light of God into every dark hearts and forming Christ inside every Christian. The kingdom of God is when other lords are dethroned from our hearts and Christ is ruling and reigning there without any contention.

"Lord, thou wilt ordain peace for us: for thou also hast wrought all our works in us". - Isaiah 26:12.

The true kingdom of God is not in eating, drinking, dancing, enjoyment and carnal pleasures but in righteousness, peace and joy in the Holy Spirit. It demonstrates itself with peace like a river in the soul, righteousness in living and unspeakable joy that radiates in our faces through the Holy Spirit of God.

The kingdom of God is the rule and reign of God in the heart of His people.

You are in the kingdom when you have peace with God, live in peace with others, and hate evil but love righteousness and full of joy that is contagious. And this can only be in your life through the Holy Spirit of God.

The sole work of the Holy Spirit in the world is to expand and extend the frontiers of God's kingdom into every heart. The Holy Spirit has been working assiduously over the centuries to establish the Kingdom of God in the hearts of men and expand it to every tribe, tongue and people.

The Holy Spirit is here to dethrone every other kingdom and lordship in the hearts of men. If you check very well, you will discover that all the empires, kingdoms, potentates and rulership of men over the ages have come and gone, only His kingdom have stood the test of time.

> **"In his days shall the righteous flourish; and abundance of peace so long as the moon endureth. He shall have dominion also from sea to sea, and from the river unto the ends of the earth. They that dwell in the wilderness shall bow before him; and his enemies shall lick the dust. The kings of Tarshish and of the isles shall bring presents: the kings of Sheba and Seba shall offer gifts. Yea, all kings shall fall down before him: all nations shall serve him. His name shall endure for ever: his name shall be continued as long as the sun: and men shall be blessed in him: all nations shall call him blessed."** - Psalm 72:7-11, 17.

The Holy Spirit is here to eradicate the kingdom of Satan, signified by sin, sickness, diseases, poverty, bad-luck, calamities, injustices and corruptions. He is working quietly through His chosen people to bring the kingdom of God into every heart.

It is your responsibility as a child of God to work with the Holy Spirit to expand and extend the kingdom of God into every heart. You must become a citizen of the kingdom. Live the life of kingdom people and preach the kingdom gospel. Dethrone every other kingdom in your heart. Build His kingdom, not your own empire and allow the Holy Spirit to work through you to destroy the kingdom of Satan in every heart you come across. Let your work, gifts and ministry expand and extend the kingdom of God into every heart. Your daily prayer must be, Lord, let your kingdom come, first into my heart and the heart of others.

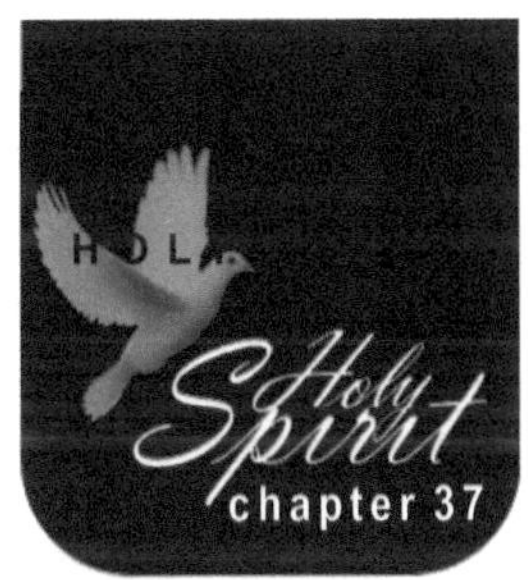

THE HOLY SPIRIT AND OBEDIENCE

❝And we are his witnesses of these things; and so is also the Holy Ghost, whom God hath given to them that obey him." - Acts 5:32

A certain brother was about going out in the morning. After praying for God's guidance, he heard the voice of the Holy Spirit telling him not to take a particular road when going with his Motorcycle. But he chose to ignore that voice speaking in his heart. He took the route in disobedience and he had a ghastly accident that he regretted for months and years.

Disobedience is a great quencher of the Holy Spirit in our lives. The Lord gives His Holy Spirit to those who obey Him. Your obedient living to the word and will of God is what will make the Holy Spirit to abide with you and give you guidance. But when you have a penchant to disobey and ignore the leadings of the Holy Spirit, you are courting trouble and disaster.

A Pastor was asked to pray with other seven Pastors through the revelations of the Holy Spirit so as to avoid serious sickness in his new pastorate. He disdained the voice of the Lord and months later he contacted a terminal sickness that terminated his life and ministry few years later.

Disobedience to the leading of the Holy Spirit is a terrible thing any Christian can do.

Another brother was instructed by the Lord not to marry a girl he proposed to marry. But he disobeyed the voice of the Lord and went ahead to marry her few days later. Well, she never gave birth in the 10 years they were married and she eventually packed out after she has scattered the church with her immoral antics. That beloved brother has not been able to pick up the pieces of his ministry till date (I Sam. 15:22-23). Disobedience is tantamount to witchcraft and idolatry.

"And Samuel said, Hath the Lord as great delight in burnt offerings and sacrifices, as in obeying the voice of the Lord? Behold, to obey is better than sacrifice, and to hearken than the fat of rams. For rebellion is as the sin of witchcraft, and stubbornness is as iniquity and idolatry. Because thou hast rejected the word of the Lord, he hath also rejected thee from being king." - 1 Samuel 15:22-23

Disobedience to the leading of the Holy Spirit is a terrible thing any Christian can do (Psalm 81:13-16). It brings darkness, confusion and bewilderment to the heart. And repeated disobedience leads to fiery judgment and indignation.

By disobedience, angels lost heaven; Satan lost his exalted positions; Adam lost Eden, Saul lost his crown and man lost his soul. I beg you in the name of the Lord, run away from disobedience, no matter how little. It is better to obey the Lord than to regret not obeying.

Firstly, you must study and pray to know the clear voice of the Holy Spirit when He is speaking. It takes maturity, but you must know His voice from the other voices of Satan and your flesh.

Secondly, you must seek to obey Him in everything. As He leads you and directs your steps, ask for grace to obey and carry out his instructions. I have heard stories of people that the Lord is calling to ministry work but was stubborn with the Lord for many years. By the time they eventually obeyed the Lord; their ministries were not as glorious as it should have been.

Please, learn to obey the Lord. Ask for His leading and obey His instructions. Though I still need to learn much more obedience, yet I can say boldly but with utmost humility that the level our ministry is today is due principally to obedience to the leadings, inspirations and voices of the Holy Spirit. Every step of obedience brings more glory to your life and every disobedience diminishes you and your ministry.

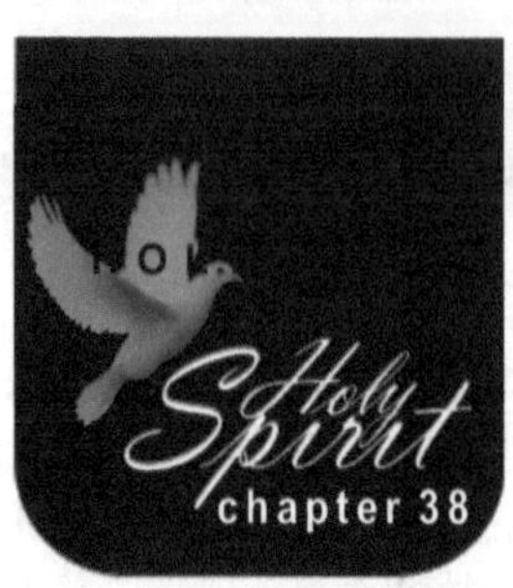

ANOINTING AND THE ANOINTED

❝❝But my horn shalt thou exalt like the horn of an unicorn: I shall be anointed with fresh oil.” - Psalm 92:10

”I have found David my servant; with my holy oil have I anointed him:” – Psalm 89:20

In the last couple of years, the subject of the anointing and the anointed has been bastardized so much. There had been lots of wrong teachings that emphasized that anointing alone is all you need in ministry and when you are anointed, nothing will be impossible unto you and you can do everything you want to do.

Furthermore, the wide spread error says that you can use the anointing to do anything and if you are anointed, your lifestyle doesn't really matter, because nobody should or must touch the Lord's anointed. The adverse effect is that these wrong teachings have made many Pentecostal and Charismatic Christians and ministers to live waywardly, seek after strange experiences and behave anyhow in the name of being anointed.

The true anointing of the Holy Spirit can be described as the unction, presence and divine enablement of the Holy Spirit upon and in a clean, dedicated and wholly obedient vessel of the Lord. The anointed is someone who is truly saved, knows the Lord intimately and whose heart and life is pleasing unto the Lord in every area.

The anointing and the anointed goes together. The anointed must be an unhindered, uncontaminated and open channel for the Holy Spirit to flow through. The anointed will be okay as long as he doesn't use the Holy Spirit, but rather allows the Holy Spirit to use him for the glory of the Lord. The anointing can be lost through sin, disobedience and indulgence. Anointing must be kept fresh and renewed always.

God will only anoint you for what He has called you to do. Anointing can grow stale and be lost. Yesterday's anointing is not and will never be sufficient for today. Anointing doesn't make you reckless nor stupid. It is not the true anointing of the Holy Spirit that makes you do stupid and foolish things in life and ministry. The anointed must live holy, pure, tender and obedient lives, if they are to keep the anointing in their lives.

"But unto the Son he saith, Thy throne, O God, is for ever and ever: a sceptre of righteousness is the sceptre of thy kingdom. Thou hast loved righteousness, and hated iniquity; therefore God, even thy God, hath anointed thee with the oil of gladness above thy fellows." – Hebrew 1:8-9.

The more obedient and consistent you are to the Lord, the more you can experience these dimensions of anointing in your life:

Magnetic anointing – Matthew 3:1,5
Mobilization anointing – Judges 6:34; Acts 6:1,4
Promotional anointing – I Sam. 16:13; Luke 4:14-15
Protectional anointing – Judges 15:14-15; I King 1:8-10
Provisional anointing – II Kings 4:1-6; Psalm 23:5
Anointing for favour – I Sam. 18:16; Luke 4:15
Everlasting anointing – II Kings 13:20-21.

Where there is the Holy Spirit propelled anointing, there can be no annoyance. These levels of anointing are necessary for resounding success in ministry. They put the devil where he belongs and place the anointed as a vanguard of recovery and restoration for humanity.

"But truly I am full of power by the spirit of the LORD, and of judgment, and of might, to declare unto Jacob his transgression, and to Israel his sin." – Micah 3:8

"Then he answered and spake unto me, saying, This is the word of the LORD unto Zerubbabel, saying, Not by might, nor by power, but by my spirit, saith the LORD of hosts." – Zechariah 4:6

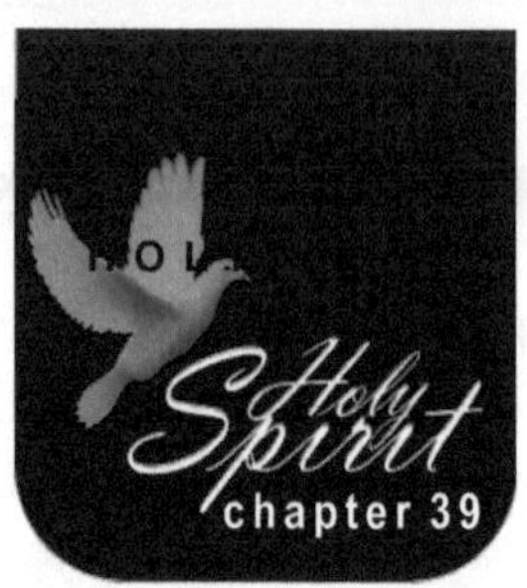

WHAT THE SPIRIT IS SAYING TO THE CHURCHES TODAY

Our Lord Jesus, the Head, Founder and Foundation of the church appeared to John the beloved in the Isle of Patmos and sent messages to the seven churches of Asia Minor. The seven churches were physical and symbolical. Seven in the scripture means perfection. So, the messages were to the seven churches then and churches of all ages. Therefore the messages were also for churches of today.

"He that hath an ear, let him hear what the Spirit saith unto the churches; To him that overcometh will I give to eat of the tree of life, which is in the midst of the paradise of God. He that hath an ear, let him hear what the Spirit saith unto the churches; He that overcometh shall not be hurt of the second death. He that hath an ear, let him hear what the Spirit saith unto the churches; To him that overcometh will I give to eat of

the hidden manna, and will give him a white stone, and in the stone a new name written, which no man knoweth saving he that receiveth it. He that hath an ear, let him hear what the Spirit saith unto the churches." – Revelation 2:7, 11, 17, 29.

"He that hath an ear, let him hear what the Spirit saith unto the churches. He that hath an ear, let him hear what the Spirit saith unto the churches. He that hath an ear, let him hear what the Spirit saith unto the churches." – Revelation 3:6, 13, 22.

He spoke to those seven churches then and He still speaks to churches today. The big question however is, are we in the right position to hear His voice to our churches today? Unfortunately, lots of churches have dull ears and cannot hear the voice of the Spirit for their churches.

Lots of churches have dull ears and cannot hear the voice of the Spirit for their churches.

"(According as it is written, God hath given them the spirit of slumber, eyes that they should not see, and ears that they should not hear;) unto this day." – Romans 11:8

"For the LORD hath poured out upon you the spirit of deep sleep, and hath closed

**your eyes: the prophets and your rulers,
the seers hath he covered."** - Isaiah 29:10

Here are the conditions of the churches then and the Spirit spoke to correct them:

1.   **Ephesian Church** – Rev. 2:1-7.
An active but formal and loveless church; doctrinal correctness but legalistic church. This is the condition of many holiness, fundamental and conservative churches today.

2.   **Smyrna Church** – Rev. 2:8-11.
A persecuted but victorious church. Examples are churches in Sudan, Northern Nigeria, Middle East, Asia, China and North Korea. External persecutions don't kill churches, but internal persecution does.

3.   **Pergamos Church** – Rev. 2:12-17
The Church with false doctrine and demonic activities. Internal collision with sin and Satan to render the church powerless from within. The case with many Traditional, Pentecostal and Charismatic churches today.

4.   **Thyatira Church** – Rev. 2:18-29
A church with sin, corruption and idolatry. Immoral preachers, conformity with the world and idolatry. Lots of Evangelical, Pentecostal and Prosperity churches are in this condition today.

5.   **Sadis Church** – Rev. 3:1-6.
The lifeless and dead church. Denominational, indigenous and missionary churches are neck deep in this condition today.

6.   **Philadelphia Church** – Rev. 3:7-13.
Faithful, loyal and godly church. Healthy, growing, quality and quantity spirituality in this church that Jesus loved.

7.   **Laodicean Church** – Rev. 3:14-22.
Worldly, carnal, lukewarm and backsliding church. Faith, prosperity and family churches are found in this condition today.

The Spirit was deeply moved at the condition of so many local branches of His church then and He spoke to them. He is still concerned with the conditions of the churches today. He is acutely aware that when the church is not what it should be, the enemy is rejoicing and sinners will keep dying and perishing. The Spirit is therefore speaking to the churches to wake up to their conditions and repent, return and renew where necessary.

The Holy Spirit gave a critical analysis, survey and down to earth solution to the seven churches then and He is still doing it now. Looking over the commands of the Spirit to those churches then, we can deduce the following as His voice to the various churches of every affiliations today:

*   He wants an active, loving, vibrant and dynamic church in the things of God.

*   He wants a glorious, spotless and wrinkleless church in all areas.

*   He wants a faithful, loyal and victorious church.

*   He wants a broken, pliable, tender and God-seeking church.

*   He wants a church free from false doctrine, idolatry, sin and demonic dominance.

*   He wants a church free from immorality and immoral ministers.

*   He wants a church steadfast and grounded in the truth.

*   He hates coldness, formality, lifeless and powerless activities in His church.

*   He wants a red-hot, fire-spitting and dynamic living church.

*   He wants a church balanced in both spiritual and maternal riches.

*   He wants a church that is steadfast in the word and prayers.

*   He wants a militant, aggressive and uncompromising church.

*   He wants a church that seeks for constant restoration, renewal, restitution and reappraisal of her relationship with God.

Can we have the anointed ears to hear the voice of the Holy Spirit to build our churches according to these desires of God? Until we hear His voice and build with Him, our churches will continue to flounder and die.

FINAL WORD

❝And whosoever speaketh a word against the Son of man, it shall be forgiven him: but whosoever speaketh against the Holy Ghost, it shall not be forgiven him, neither in this world, neither in the world to come. Either make the tree good, and his fruit good; or else make the tree corrupt, and his fruit corrupt: for the tree is known by his fruit.❞ - Matthew 12:32-33

Our Lord Jesus elevates the Holy Spirit to deity status in His comments here. He says every blasphemy against Him will be forgiven but against the Holy Spirit is unforgivable. How great and profound is the person, power and divinity of the Holy Spirit then?

Thou Spirit of the Lord, help me never to blaspheme you in my life! To blaspheme against the Holy Spirit is first and foremost, not to recognize Him and detest His presence and power. And there are lots of professed Christians today who are too proud, cocky and educated to acknowledge the greater wisdom, knowledge, power and leadership of the Holy Spirit both in the church and in their lives.

Secondly, to blaspheme against the Holy Spirit is to ascribe His work to the devil. Lots of ignorant, carnal and spiritually blind people are doing just that today. Simply because there had been false miracles by false prophets, they now refuse to believe the genuine work of the Holy Spirit because it's not happening through their instrumentalities.

Thirdly, to blaspheme the Holy Spirit is to use occultic and demonic powers to perform spurious miracles and yet ascribe them to the work of the Holy Spirit of God, and lots of preachers are doing that today. In the pressure to perform, make money and be relevant, they have gone for fake miracles, just to deceive and enrich their pockets. Yet, they come to the public to say God the Holy Spirit is the one doing those things. What a height of blasphemy against the Lord!

Well, Jesus says the Holy Spirit will not spare such people. I beg you in the name of the Lord; welcome the Holy Spirit back into your heart and life through genuine repentance and humility. Don't ever blaspheme Him, because He is the true Vicar that is nurturing the church here and will take the church home.

Dear Holy Spirit of God, welcome back to our lives and churches afresh! Take the pre-eminence in all things! For without you, we are nothing!

BIBLIOGRAPHY

1. Unpublished lecture notes on the Holy Spirit by Francis Bola Akin-John – 1991

2. Unpublished lecture notes on the Holy Spirit by Francis Bola Akin-John – 2005

3. Conference lecture notes by Francis Bola Akin-John – 2010.

INTERNATIONAL CHURCH GROWTH MINISTRIES

INTERNATIONAL CHURCH GROWTH MINISTRY was founded in 1994. The vision of the ministry is to provide current and reliable Church Growth principles in African context to Leaders, Pastors and Ministers that will lead to better and faster growth of their churches.

We do these through books, materials, VCD and audio cassettes at relatively low cost to people engaged in leading the church.

We equally organise seminars and conferences on various aspect of Church Growth and Health. We also accept invitations from churches to help analyse them, motivate their people and generally help the growth potentials of churches.

So far we have ministered to over 20,000 Pastors and Christian Workers across many denominational lines and independent churches. The results have been tremendous and the testimonies have been wonderful and interesting.

The ministry also saw the need to really raise the growth consciousness in the Continent and decided to pioneer an Institute on Church Growth. The response has been overwhelming as so many Pastors, General Overseers, and Church Leaders have enrolled to learn more about how to practically lead their churches to growth. The impact of the Institute on these Pastors' lives have started manifesting in the phenomenal growth of their churches and expansion of their ministries.

ICGM RESOURCES

If you found this book to be useful, you may be interested in some of the other books and resources produced by ICGM. Listed below are:

THE BOOKS:
1. How To Support And Strengthen Your Pastors
2. Pulpit Power For Church Growth
3. Your Growth Is Your Future
4. The Secrets Of Financially Strong Churches
5. Closing The Back Door Of Your Churches
6. Spiritual Warfare And Church Growth
7. 40 Strategic Ways To Increase Church Attendance
8. Supernatural Power, Miracles, Signs & Wonders Today
9. Our Churches And His Church
10. Strategic Living
11. Leading Your Church To Lasting Growth
12. 22 Dynamic Laws Of Church Growth
13. Strategic Church Planting Today
14. The Place Of Anointing And Administration
15. The Impact Driven Church
16. Grow The Pastor, Grow The Church
17. Personal Growth Today

TEACHING RESOURCES:

33. Effective Pastors For Today
34. A Well-equipped, Competent, Matured & Healthy Pastoral Leader Of Today
35. Viable Church Planting & Healthy Church Growth
36. Great Leaders, Great Ministries
37. Empowering The Church For 21st Century
38. Secrets Of Successful Churches, Significant Ministries & Supernatural Ministers
39. Leadership Without Limitation
40. Relevant & Resourceful Ministers
41. Church Without Walls
42. Healthy Leadership For Healthy Churches
43. Tools For Tremendous And Transforming Ministry.
44. New Waves Of God's Move For End Time Harvest
45. Magnetic, Multiplying, Marketable And Maximum Impact.
46. Building A Bigger, Better And Broader Church And Many Others
47. High Impact Church In Every Community
48. Difference-making Church/ministry
49. Church Overseers Course Series
50. Church Workers Congress Series
51. Real Man Seminar Series

And many more.

AUDIO TAPES, CD, VCD & MP3
All our seminars and conferences messages.

JOURNAL:
Church Growth Journal is a quarterly teaching and news magazine that gives vital and practical information on how to grow the church.

For further information on these and other resources available, please write or contact us at our office or call the telephone lines provided in this book.

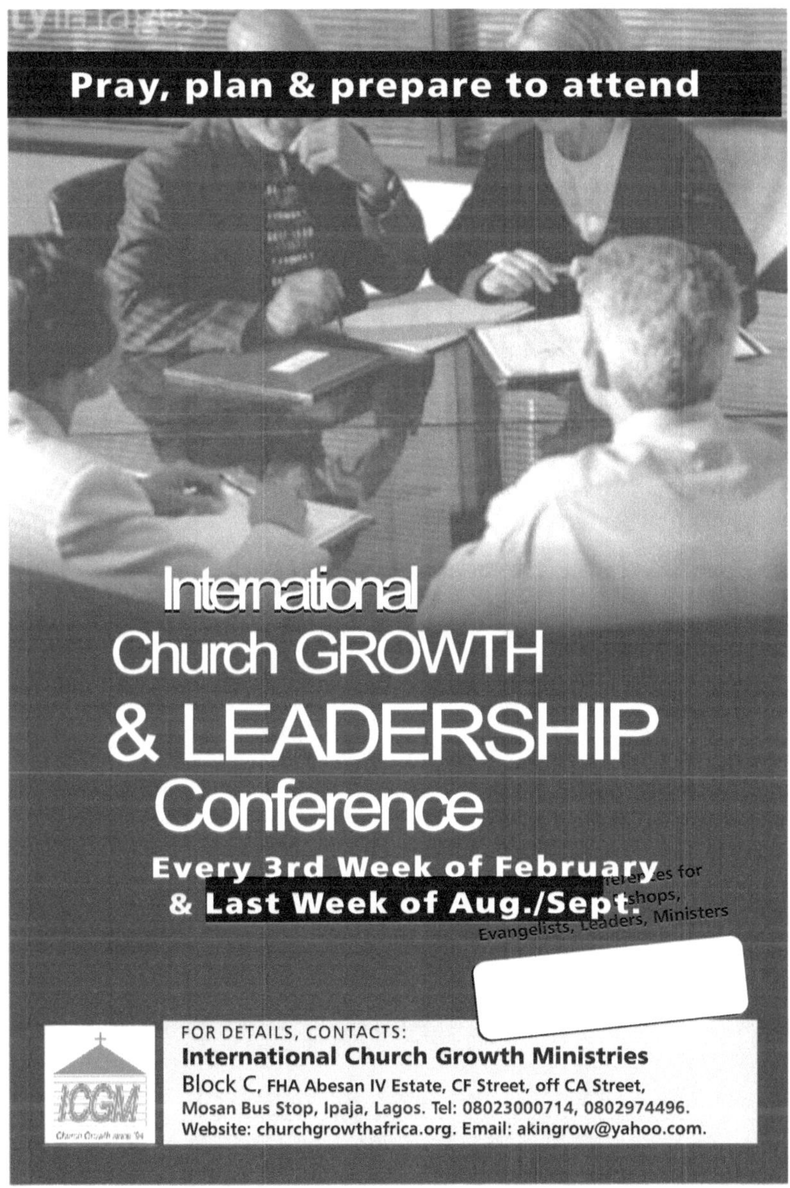
Pray, plan & prepare to attend
International
Church GROWTH
& LEADERSHIP
Conference
Every 3rd Week of February
& Last Week of Aug./Sept.
Evangelists, Leaders, Ministers
FOR DETAILS, CONTACTS:
International Church Growth Ministries
Block C, FHA Abesan IV Estate, CF Street, off CA Street,
Mosan Bus Stop, Ipaja, Lagos. Tel: 08023000714, 0802974496.
Website: churchgrowthafrica.org. Email: akingrow@yahoo.com.
ICGM

Dr. Francis Bola
AKIN-JOHN

* Started ministry in 1988.
* Pastored five denominational churches in the space of 8 years.
* Started Church Growth Ministry in 1994 after hearing God said "Go and strengthen pastors and support churches to grow and be healthy".
* Has held hundreds of conferences across Nigeria, Africa and Europe with combined attendance of many Thousands of church leaders.
* Has written over 35 books that has sold thousands of copies such as 'Grow the Pastor, Grow the Church', 'The Impact-Driven Church', and '22 Dynamic Laws of Church Growth'.
* Founded International Institute of Church Growth that has trained over 5,000 pastors and leaders with attendant growth testimonies.
* Has written and produced hundreds of materials on various aspects of church growth, leadership and health that is being used by thousands of church leaders.
* Has mobilized and equipped men to become real men through seminars, resources and tapes.
* Has sold thousands of tapes - audio, DVD, CDs that continued to bless and edify thousands of ministers and church leaders.
* Has consulted and helped many denominational and independent churches to overcome stagnation, crisis and breakaways.
* Has been used by God to raise and grow thousands of ministers, churches and ministries across the nations.
* He is trying to live his major passion of "Empowering Leaders to Grow Healthier Churches and Ministries" across the world.